GREAT ART AND ARTISTS OF THE WORLD

IMPRESSIONISTS AND POST-IMPRESSIONISTS

IMPRESSIONISTS AND POST-IMPRESSIONISTS

Edited, with an Introduction, by
Alan Bowness
Lecturer in History of Art, Courtauld Institute of Art, London

FRANKLIN WATTS, INC.
A Division of Grolier Incorporated
575 LEXINGTON AVENUE, NEW YORK 10022

HOW TO USE THIS BOOK

To obtain the maximum information and interest from this series it is necessary to understand its basic plan. With the exception of the first volume and the last two volumes, which are more general in their scope, each of the other seven volumes is arranged as follows:

First, a historical Introduction sets out the main lines of development within the school or period, with special reference to the major artists and the major works of art.

This is followed by a biographical section outlining the life and work of every major artist and important minor artists. The Biographies run in alphabetical order according to the name by which each artist is most generally known, whether it be surname, or Christian name (as for example LEONARDO da Vinci), or nickname (as TINTORETTO). With each biography is given a cross-reference to the page or pages on which he is represented in the plates sections which follow; a monochrome reproduction of one or more of his other works; and (where possible) a self-portrait or portrait of the artist and a specimen of his signature.

Next follow the sections of Color Plates, Drawings, and Sculpture. Each of these sections is arranged in chronological order according to the date of the artist's birth, though in a few cases minor adjustments to this order have been made for the sake of comparison or design. To illustrate painting techniques, particularly of frescoes and large easel paintings, some color plates show a detail rather than the whole work; but the use of such a detail is indicated in the caption, and a monochrome illustration of the whole work is normally given with the artist's biography; in such cases the size given in the caption refers to the whole painting. The location of every work of art is included in its caption. Every effort has been made to include also the size, medium, and date of each work represented in the plates, though this has not always been possible since not every museum has such information available for all the items in its collection. The reader will also appreciate that the precise dating of many works of art is the subject of scholarly controversy; however, no dates have been included here unless they have the authority of qualified experts and art historians.

A final section, entitled Influences and Developments, rounds off the period by drawing together the main ideas and characteristics of schools and styles, and by exploring the internal and external influences that have made their impact on the development of the arts during the period concerned.

A list of basic reference books for further reading appears on page 16. Books containing material of special interest concerning an individual artist are listed at the end of the relevant biography.

To avoid repetitive explanation of basic technical terms such as *genre, chiaroscuro, baroque*, etc., an illustrated Glossary is provided in the volume entitled *How to Look at Art*. Also in that volume is an Index listing every artist mentioned throughout the series.

Taken as a whole, the series thus provides a comprehensive, carefully integrated, and highly informative survey of the achievement and significance of Western Art from its origins to the present day.

NOTE.—The terminal dates in the titles of some of the volumes are inevitably approximate. One volume will sometimes overlap with another. Some artists mentioned under French Art, for example, are also represented under the Impressionists, and the Post-Impressionists merge imperceptibly with the Moderns. In the ever-continuous process of Art it is difficult to contain schools or periods within precise boundaries.

Library of Congress Catalog Card Number: 65-10269
Copyright © 1965 by Grolier Incorporated
Also published 1965 by Grolier Incorporated under the title of *The Book of Art*

Designed and produced by George Rainbird Ltd., London
PRINTED IN ITALY by Amilcare Pizzi S.p.A., Milan

Contents

ACKNOWLEDGMENTS

The publishers and producers wish to express their gratitude to all the museums, art galleries, collectors, photographers, and agencies who have courteously assisted them in obtaining the material for the illustrations reproduced in this volume. They would especially like to thank the following:

The Addison Gallery of American Art, Phillips Academy, Andover, Mass.
Albertina, Vienna
The Albright-Knox Art Gallery, Buffalo, N.Y.
The Allen Memorial Art Museum, Oberlin College, Oberlin, Ohio
The Art Institute, Chicago
The Art Gallery, Gothenburg, Sweden
The Arts Council of Great Britain, London
The Ashmolean Museum, Oxford
The Barnes Foundation, Merion, Pa.
Bibliothèque Nationale, Paris
Joachim Blauel, Munich
Mr. and Mrs. Leigh B. Block, Chicago
Boymans-van Beuningen Museum, Rotterdam
The Trustees of the British Museum, London
Mr. J. N. Brown, Newport, Rhode Island
The Bührle Collection, Zurich
The Burrell Collection, Glasgow, Art Gallery

Monsieur J. Camponogara, Lyon
Centraal Museum, Utrecht
Château de Rohan, Strasbourg
Mr. Walter P. Chrysler, Jr., New York
The City Art Gallery, Manchester, England
The City Art Museum, St. Louis, Mo.
The City Museum and Art Gallery, Birmingham, England
The Courtauld Institute Galleries, London
The Courtauld Institute of Art, London
Mr. Walter Dräyer, Zurich
Durand-Ruel and Cie., Paris
Lord Farington, Buscot Park, Berkshire, England
The Fitzwilliam Museum, Cambridge, England
Mr. and Mrs. L. A. Fleischman, Detroit
R. B. Fleming and Co. Ltd., London
The Fogg Art Museum, Cambridge, Mass.
The Folkwang Museum, Essen
John R. Freeman and Co., London
The Freer Gallery of Art, Washington, D.C.
Gallerie Civica d'Arte Moderna, Milan
Gallerie Nazionale d'Arte Moderna, Rome
The Gallery of Modern Art, New York
Gayroma Ltd., Wolverhampton, England
Gemäldegalerie, Dresden
Gemäldesammlung, Essen

V. W. van Gogh Collection, Stedelijk Museum, Amsterdam
The Herron Museum of Art, Indianapolis
Colorphoto Hans Hinz, SWB, Basel
The Institute of Arts, Detroit
Jefferson Medical College, Philadelphia, Pa.
John G. Johnson Collection, Philadelphia, Pa.
Kunsthalle, Bremen
Kunsthalle, Hamburg
Kunsthaus, Zurich
Kunstmuseum, Bern
Kupferstichkabinett, Basel
The Lefevre Gallery, London
The Louvre, Paris
Mr. Wright Ludington, Santa Barbara, Calif.
M. Dominique Maurice-Denis, Saint-Germain-en-Laye, France
The Metropolitan Museum of Art, New York
Munch-Museet, Oslo
Musée, Albi
Musée Bourdelle, Paris
Musée de l'Impressionnisme, Paris
Musée de Picardie, Amiens
Musée de Rennes, Rennes
Musée des Beaux-Arts, Algiers
Musée des Beaux-Arts, Amiens
Musée des Beaux-Arts, Cherbourg
Musée des Beaux-Arts, Le Havre
Musée des Beaux-Arts, Lille
Musée des Beaux-Arts, Lyon
Musée des Beaux-Arts, Nantes
Musée des Beaux-Arts, Pau
Musée des Beaux-Arts, Reims
Musée du Petit-Palais, Paris
Musée Ensor, Ostend
Musée Gustave Moreau, Paris
Musée Marmottan, Paris
Musée National d'Art Moderne, Paris
Musée Rodin, Paris
Musée Royal des Beaux-Arts, Antwerp
Musées Royaux des Beaux-Arts, Brussels
The Museum, Malmö
The Museum, Newcastle-on-Tyne, England
The Museum and Art Gallery, São Paolo
The Museum of Art, Baltimore, Md.
The Museum of Art, Cleveland, Ohio
The Museum of Art, Philadelphia, Pa.
The Museum of Art, Toledo, Ohio
The Museum of Fine Arts, Boston, Mass.

The Museum of Fine Arts, Leipzig
The Museum of Modern Art, New York
The Museum of Modern Western Art, Moscow
Národni Vladimir Fyman, Prague
Nasjonalgalleriet, Oslo
The Trustees of the National Gallery, London
The National Gallery of Art, Washington, D.C.
The National Gallery of Canada, Ottawa
The National Gallery of Scotland, Edinburgh
The National Museum of Wales, Cardiff
The National Trust, London
Nationalmuseum, Stockholm
Neue Pinakothek, Munich
Ny Carlsberg Glyptothek, Copenhagen
Öffentliche Kunstsammlung, Basel
The Phillips Collection, Washington, D.C.
Photographie Giraudon, Paris
Mr. and Mrs. J. Pulitzer, Jr., St. Louis, Mo.
The Oskar Reinhardt Collection, Winterthur, Switzerland
Gerhard Reinhold, Leipzig
The Royal Holloway College, Egham, Surrey, England
Österreichische Galerie, Vienna
The Rhode Island School of Design, Providence
Rijksmuseum Kröller-Müller, Otterlo, Holland
Colonel Sands, East House, Oxfordshire, England
Smith College, Northampton, Mass.
The Society of Fine Arts, Wilmington, Del.
Société Guerlain, Paris
The Solomon R. Guggenheim Museum Collection, New York
Staatliche Museen, West Berlin
Städelsches Kunstinstitut, Frankfurt-am-Main
Städtische Kunsthalle, Mannheim
Städtisches Museum, Wuppertal
Stedelijk Museum, Amsterdam
The Taft Museum, Cincinnati, Ohio
The Trustees of the Tate Gallery, London
Armand Tornow, São Paolo
The Uffizi Gallery, Florence
The University of Pennsylvania, Philadelphia, Pa.
The Victoria and Albert Museum (Crown Copyright), London
The Wadsworth Atheneum, Hartford, Conn.
The Walker Art Gallery, Liverpool, England
Wallraf-Richartz-Museum, Cologne
John Hay Whitney Collection, New York
Wildenstein Inc., New York
The William Rockhill Nelson Gallery of Art, Kansas City
The Yale University Art Gallery, New Haven, Conn.
The Zoological Institute, Naples

ABBREVIATIONS

et al.	and elsewhere
in.	inches
St.	Saint
S.	Saint (Italian)
Acad.	Academie
B-A.	Beaux-Arts
Bibl.	Bibliothèque
B. M.	British Museum
Coll.	Collection
Gal.	Galerie
Gall.	Galleria, Galleris, Gallery
Gemäldegal.	Gemäldegalerie
Inst.	Institute
Konstmus.	Konstmuseum
Kunsthist.	Kunsthistorisches
Kunstinst.	Kunstinstitut
Kunstsamm.	Kunstsammlung
Met. Mus.	Metropolitan Museum of Art, New York
Mus.	Musée, Museen, Museo, Museum
Nasjonalgall.	Nasjonalgalleriet
Nat.	Nationale
Nationalmus.	Nationalmuseum
Naz.	Nazionale
N.G.	National Gallery, London
	National Gallery of Art, Washington, D.C.
Pal.	Palais
Pin.	Pinakothek
Rijksmus.	Rijksmuseum
Staatl.	Staatliche
Städt.	Städtische
Tate	Tate Gallery, London
V. and A.	Victoria and Albert Museum, London

Impressionists and Post-Impressionists

The artist becomes independent

When does modern art begin? At which moment in the great historical progression of art does a flavor of our own time suddenly come into painting, so that we feel we are no longer looking at something that belongs to another age and civilization? Clearly the change took place in France, and in the 19th century; but claims could be made for a number of individual pictures, for it was of course no sharp and distinct break. If we look to the middle of the century, however, there is one painting that suggests a new beginning in more ways than one.

This is Courbet's *The Painter's Studio* (pp. 127 and 257), first exhibited in Paris in 1855. It is enormous, nearly twenty feet wide, and although not obviously beautiful, has a richness of design and meaning still very evident today. In it Courbet was trying to do something quite original. In order to explain his intentions he provided the picture with a strange subtitle: "real allegory summing up a seven-year period of my artistic life," and described it at length to a friend:

"The scene is laid in my studio in Paris. The picture is divided into two parts. I am in the center, painting. On the right are all the active participants—that is, my friends, the workers, the art collectors. On the left are the others—those whose lives are without significance: the common people, the destitute, the poor, the wealthy, the exploited, the exploiters, those who thrive on death."

The whole picture is, in Sir Kenneth Clark's words, "a great poem of self-love." Courbet was indeed a notorious egoist. But he was striking a blow for the independence of the artist, who here becomes the subject of his art in no uncertain manner. Since Courbet, everything and anything has been possible for the artist. For better or worse, artists have been free from the demands of society, able, even encouraged, to go their own ways and to trust that public appreciation would follow.

Courbet called his new style realism and thought of it as the final form of art. Realism was in the first place a revolution in subject matter. There were to be no more paintings of allegory, nor of events from the Bible or history or literature, for Courbet regarded ordinary people and everyday scenes and things as the only possible subjects for art. He denied the place in art of imagination: an artist, he said, is capable of representing only what he can actually see and touch; he must try to do this as simply and directly as possible. But, as Courbet was to discover, this was easier said than done. In due course it led him and his successors, particularly Monet and Cézanne, to explore the nature of perception, or how we see things, and of pictorial representation, how we can paint them.

For Courbet realized, as we see from *The Painter's Studio*, that the picture itself makes certain demands upon the artist. He disliked the careful arrangement of figures in an illusionistic setting that was conventionally regarded as "composition," but he knew that within the four sides of a picture some kind of unity must prevail. The painter's task is to create a convincing space there. This Courbet achieved by means of light and shadow, so that the many figures seem indeed to be gathered together in the same room. Colors, tone, and texture all help to unify a rather casual, and even irrational, assemblage of people. Nor did Courbet forget that a picture is a flat surface; as we shall see, the implications of this reverberate through the painting of the next fifty years.

Courbet never again attempted anything so ambitious as *The Painter's Studio*. It was his declaration of independence, but one that seems to have come near to exhausting even his considerable energies. He was unable to finish his next sizable figure composition, *The Bride's Toilet* (p. 128). We can see why. It is the boldest and most radical of all his pictures; in it he appears to distort the forms of the human body, the perspective of the room and the furniture in it. The result is quite unlike a photograph of the subject and may be regarded as "unreal." But the human eye is a much more complex instrument than the camera. We have not one aperture but two; and the eyes are always moving, exploring, bringing back information to the brain, information that the painter has to clarify and re-order on the flat surface of his picture. He does not see as the camera sees. Thus *The Bride's Toilet* comes much closer than would a photograph to recording Courbet's visual sensations of the scene.

In his later years Courbet achieved a more complete success only when he painted simple subjects: apples on a dish, a vase of flowers, a trout, a nude woman, a tree in a field, a wave breaking. Here the materiality of the painting, the rich, thick, grainy paint spread over the surface, acts as the equivalent of the thing painted, and sometimes gives it a larger-than-life quality so that the wave seems not one particular wave, but all waves and the whole movement of the sea.

Composition for its own sake

Courbet had often tried to paint a group of figures out-of-doors in a landscape, and his conspicuous lack of success inspired two younger painters in the 1860's to offer their solutions to what was at the time a considerable artistic problem. In such a fashion does art progress. The two painters were Manet and Monet, and the similarity of their names led to frequent confusion, though in their early careers they were developing in very different directions.

Édouard Manet was the older of the two by some eight years, and he succeeded Courbet in the 1860's as the leader of the *avant-garde* painters. This was not altogether to his liking, for he was by temperament no revolutionary. He regarded himself, quite rightly, as a traditionalist. He was not much troubled by a desire to record his visual sensations, nor does he appear to have attached great importance to subject matter, though we know he preferred to draw for this upon modern life. It was pictorial composition that mattered most to him, or what we might call the science of picture making.

As a painter Manet was extremely well educated: he had made a profound study of the painting of the past and did not hesitate to use his knowledge—so much so, that he has at times been unjustly accused of plagiarism. Yet he sought always a specifically modern kind of composition, one that would accord with the new feeling, first apparent in Courbet, for the essential flatness of a picture and for the fact that before all else it is an object complete and self-sufficient. Manet's *Le Déjeuner sur l'Herbe* (p. 130) and *Olympia* (p. 131), for example, contain echoes of earlier pictures, by Giorgione and Titian and Goya among others, but have an overall flavor that is quite distinct and original. Manet made his figures much flatter than those of any predecessor (Courbet called Olympia a "playing-card queen") by placing the source of light as it were in front of a picture, never at the sides. He exaggerated the contrast between light and dark, eliminating the in-between gray tones and so further flattening all the forms.

It was then easier to organize them into a pictorial composition. This Manet did with consummate mastery. The placing of every part of every painting is most beautifully accomplished, and never more apparent than in *Le Déjeuner* (p. 132). In many ways this is an artificial picture, introducing certain objects—the sword and helmet, or the peeled lemon on the table—for purely aesthetic reasons. One would not expect to find them in such a room as that portrayed; they are there because the artist wanted this or that particular shape or tone or color at this or that particular point. *Le Déjeuner* does not lack a human element, however: the boy's gaze catches our attention and—one of Manet's favorite devices—roots us to the spot immediately in front of the picture. The staring gaze was sometimes combined in Manet's work with a somewhat provocative quality. It was this that made *Le Déjeuner sur l'Herbe* and *Olympia* such a scandal and sensation.

Impressionism: recording nature and light

Claude Monet was the leader of the Impressionist group and, more than anyone, the creator of Impressionist painting. He was very unlike Manet in social background, upbringing, taste, and character. He appears to have been quite uninterested in the art of the past and regarded all theories about art with horror. His prime concern was with the recording of his visual sensations; his only desire, in his own words, was "to paint directly from nature, striving to render my impressions in the face of the most fugitive effects."

Monet began by tackling the problem, which had defeated Courbet, of painting figures in a convincing open-air setting. He would have thought Manet's solution, in *Le Déjeuner sur l'Herbe*, too composed and too confusedly lighted. Monet observed that light alone has the power of unifying figure and landscape. So he experimented by painting *Women in the Garden* (p. 141) out-of-doors and only when the sun was shining through the trees. This was the first picture faithfully to record the effect of outdoor light on the figure.

Monet's new awareness of light was to transform painting. In spirit he worked in the succession of Courbet, trying to put on to his canvas what he saw and no more. But as he soon discovered, the simpler the painter's aims, the more complicated and difficult his task becomes. During his long career—he lived to be eighty-six—Monet reduced painting to its bare essentials. He began by observing effects of light that earlier artists had never altogether succeeded in catching, particularly the reflection of the sky on the surface of water and the play of bright sunshine on water and on snow. Guided always by the evidence of his eyes, he noticed that shadows are not brown, but colored, and that things change their colors when placed in different positions or lights.

In order to record what he saw, Monet found himself employing much brighter pigments than any he had used before. Whenever possible he worked with pure, unmixed colors, the three primaries (red, yellow, blue) and their three complementaries (green, violet, orange). Blacks, browns, and earth shades soon disappeared from his pictures. As a result of this new use of color and because he wanted to reproduce the feeling of movement of quivering light, Monet's handling of paint became very free and loose; he made no attempt to disguise his brush-strokes. His works therefore looked to his contemporaries incomplete and unfinished. In 1872 he had used the word "impression" for the title of a picture, and the term "Impressionist" was now taken up and applied to all work of the same kind.

By the end of the 1870's Impressionism was an established style of painting. Monet had not been alone in his researches: among his close friends were Frédéric Bazille, who met a premature death in the Franco-Prussian war; the Englishman Alfred Sisley, who represented the link with Constable and Turner; and, most important, Auguste Renoir, who pioneered the lighter, brighter colors even before Monet. Renoir, however, did not share what soon became Monet's exclusive interest, landscape. He enjoyed painting pretty girls, and his art, like that of Manet and Degas, reflects the activities of the smart Parisian society of the day. The general air of delight and gaiety that surrounds much Impressionist painting, belying the artists' material circumstances, was due in large measure to Renoir.

Monet and his friends joined forces with other young artists who were at odds with the Salon establishment and wanted to show their work to the public. It was thus that the exhibitions of the independent group began, in 1874. These exhibitions were later called Impressionist, but the term fits the work of Monet and Renoir better than it does that of Degas, Pissarro, or Cézanne, the other leading figures in the group.

Impressionism: recording figures and movement

Edgar Degas kept an aristocratic distance. His early work was on conventional lines: large history paintings, designed for submission to the Salons, and portraits in the manner of Ingres, whom he greatly admired. In these portraits, however, the world in which the sitter lived gradually assumed more and more importance. From painting singers and musicians in the orchestra pit it was only a short step to painting dancers on the stage and in rehearsal. Degas became obsessed with the movement of figures, with catching in paint or crayon the particular moment that seems to imply both the beginning and the end of a gesture. With the same singleness of purpose that Monet showed, he restricted his subject-matter to the women who were his models, depicting them in an ever more narrow range of gestures: washing, stepping from a tub, drying themselves with a towel, combing and brushing their hair. With complete objectivity and lack of emotion or any kind of personal feeling, Degas observed. Although his detachment lent a coldness to his work, few painters can rival him in the representation of the human body.

Renoir's late work was also centered upon the human figure, but his ample and sensuous nudes express a positive feeling for life very different from the aloof view of Degas. Both painters turned to sculpture as the natural extension of their pictorial interests. It is a singular fact, reflecting on the generally poor level of this art at the time, that, with the exception of Rodin and Rosso, the best sculpture of the 19th century was produced by painters.

Renoir and all his contemporaries had passed through an artistic crisis in the 1880's, at the very moment when public recognition and financial success were coming to them. The reason for this crisis was simple: Impressionism marked the culmination of naturalistic painting. Nobody has ever succeeded in giving a more convincing representation of a landscape than Monet. A moment of perfection in the history of art had been reached. It was also a dead end.

Painting of time

Monet wanted somehow to go further. By the 1880's, so far as he was concerned, Impressionism was finished. His friends suspected that he began now to record light and atmosphere for their own sakes, indifferent to what it was that he happened to paint. Anything, in fact, seemed to serve him as a subject. The simpler (a haystack) or the more intractable (the Gothic façade of Rouen cathedral) it was, the better he liked it. Further, what really mattered to him now was the artist's own experience of changing light conditions: Monet appears to be painting not so much what he sees, as how he sees.

Time became a factor of major importance. In his desire to seize upon the exact moment of vision, Monet found himself at work on a dozen or more canvases of the same subject, each recording a particular moment in the day. The artificiality of such a procedure led him to

reflect upon the nature of time; so that in his last works, the paintings of lilies floating on water (p. 145), one seems to have gone beyond everyday reality into some strange world behind appearances, where cosmic, elemental forces are in play. These lily pond pictures slowly grew in size and took on unparalleled dimensions; composition as Monet understood it disappeared and all the forms dissolved in light. The colored brush-marks provided a new architecture for painting: the paint never vanishes into the scene it represents; it is always real and tangible on the surface of the picture, aglow with the artist's inner illumination.

Structure and space

Monet's achievement was surpassed only by one man, Paul Cézanne, who is certainly the greatest of all painters since Rembrandt. Lacking Monet's single-mindedness, Cézanne had a greater range and universality. He was personally responsible for much that is modern art; since Cézanne, painting can never be the same.

One may best explain his influence by saying that he re-thought the whole question of painting. He went back to fundamentals, taking as his starting point the problem of interpreting the three-dimensional unbounded world in terms of the two-dimensional rectangular picture. He too was very conscious of the confused nature of human perception. He sought a new way of pictorial composition that would match his own experiences. By his own standards he failed, but it is this that gives his career its tragic and heroic quality.

Cézanne abandoned from the beginning some of the tricks, such as linear perspective, that artists had used unquestioningly for centuries. His early work was consequently dismissed as childish; and as he was a man of strong feelings, which he wished to transmit through his paintings, it was often overcharged with his private emotions. Realizing this, he deliberately went to school with Camille Pissarro for a time in the early 1870's, in order to learn from him the Impressionist use of paint and color, and light and space. But the momentary effects of Impressionism were not what Cézanne wanted in painting. They were too superficial, too impermanent. He sought to penetrate beneath appearances, in order to make pictorial reconstructions of what he called his "sensations before nature."

The results were some of the most original pictures ever painted. Because he was constantly analyzing his own sensations, Cézanne knew that the eye is always on the move, seeing round things, exploring deep into space. In his pictures he may combine several "viewpoints" or eye levels, and thus by implication successive moments of time. We look at his pictures in time, not at a glance: our eyes play over them, as they do over the real world of appearances. We have here something more permanent and informative than a snapshot.

In his work of the 1880's Cézanne seems to be looking for regular shapes that may be found underneath everything that we see—the hidden architecture of things. These paintings have a solidity that later disappeared, when Cézanne realized that space could be known only in and through time; he would have to take into account the ever-changing consciousness of the observer. As we have seen, this was also Monet's experience. It can be paralleled in near-contemporary developments in science (Einstein), philosophy (Bergson), and the other arts (Debussy, Mallarmé, Proust).

The consequence in Cézanne's work was an ever-increasing integration of means, until it becomes impossible to separate modeling, drawing, color, tone, composition. The colored brush-stroke, as in Monet, is the all-important common denominator: bold, squarish marks on the canvas, which are so exactly right in shape and color that they immediately take up a position in space, and can be "read" as a mountain-side or the plane of a cheek or whatever it is they happen to represent. The whole picture is alive and unified, caught up in some universal rhythm of creation. For, as in Monet's late work, the color seems to spring from the depths of nature.

Cézanne himself said: "I sometimes imagine colors as great noumenal entities, living ideas, beings of pure reason." It is as if, after years of recording the appearances of things, he came close to the thing in itself, which is essentially unknown and unknowable. No words can explain the mystery and grandeur of the late paintings and when the landscape is filled with figures it is like an image of some ideal existence.

Color and composition systematized

Neither Monet nor Cézanne reached the climax of their achievements until the turn of the century. Meanwhile younger painters, all of whom predeceased them, took the art of painting in entirely new directions. As we have seen, there was a general crisis in Impressionist circles in the 1880's, when the knowledge dawned that straightforward naturalism was exhausted and could now only be vulgarized. Naturalism was in any case coming to be equated with materialism, and as the century drew to its close so did the more questing minds start to doubt the values on which society was based. A concentration on artistic problems alone did not seem sufficient. It was against this background that the Post-Impressionist reaction occurred. There were two rival but often related movements, led by Seurat and Gauguin. Van Gogh, the greatest of the three Post-Impressionists, drew from both the others and went his own way.

Georges Seurat brought to painting the brilliant logic of a mathematician, anxious to clarify and tabulate. He analyzed the roles in painting first of tone, then of color and finally of line and composition, proposing a kind of scientific Impressionism. He concentrated his researches in ambitious figure compositions, such as *Une Baignade* (p. 162) and *A Sunday Afternoon on the Island of La Grande Jatte* (p. 163), that he prepared with immense care. *La Grande Jatte*, for example, took him the best part of two years: he made over thirty small oil studies for the composition and almost as many drawings of individual figures. Seurat was an extremely methodical man. In making a system out of the Impressionist technique he reduced brush-strokes to dots of paint and, at one stage, used only the three primary colors and their complementaries.

Space within his pictures became more and more shallow. In the last large painting, the strangely colored *Circus* (p. 165), the design is entirely on the surface, like a poster. Seurat did all he could to emphasize its flatness. There is very little modeling and no linear perspective. The eye moves up and down the picture, so that we seem to be on a level with figures at both the top and the bottom. All this enabled Seurat to concentrate on the pictorial construction, which he worked out with mathematical exactitude, making use of such ancient and half-magical formulas as the Golden Mean, the division of a line according to the proportion most harmonious to the eye.

Seurat's early death at the age of thirty-one was a tragedy. At the end of his life he was evolving a theory according to which moods of joy, serenity, and sadness can be directly conveyed in terms of tone, color, and line. Subject matter now played a very subservient part. The way lay open, as in so much late 19th-century painting, for a completely abstract art.

The artist as rebel and visionary

With Seurat, Impressionism was brought to a kind of symbolism. Something similar happened in the work of Paul Gauguin. As early as 1885 Gauguin was interested in the significance of lines, numbers, colors, and shapes, but it was not until 1888 that he finally broke with Impressionism and with what he called the "gross error of naturalism." The first picture in the new style, *The Vision after the Sermon* (p. 166), was of Breton women who, coming from Mass, have a vision of Jacob struggling with the angel. Gauguin felt free to introduce into his painting an element of unreality. His choice of form and color was arbitrary, or, rather, made for expressive reasons. He used flat areas of bright color with heavy enclosing lines because this helped to stress the primitive, naive quality that he wished all art to possess.

In him we meet the artist in complete opposition to society. Courbet's declaration of artistic independence had resulted in Gauguin's attitude of artistic defiance. Gauguin detested the European society of his day. He found it overcivilized and decadent and thought all its values wrong. Through his art he sought to offer an alternative. He chose to live among the most simple and unspoiled people that he could find, at first in Brittany and then in Tahiti and the Marquesas Islands, and he painted them in a style that matched his subject. To create this style, sometimes called Symbolist, he drew upon non-European art sources, notably Japanese prints and Oriental and primitive sculpture, for he knew that an infusion of the kind was necessary for the revivification of western European art. He was right. He helped to create the climate of thought that made appreciation of artists like Henri Rousseau possible, and his own

innovations led directly to the immense stylistic variety of 20th-century art.

Gauguin had parted company with Impressionist painters such as Pissarro, his teacher as well as Cézanne's, on the grounds that "they seek around the eye, and not at the mysterious centers of thought." He was in no way concerned with the pursuit of appearances. The recording of the experience of seeing that obsessed Monet and Cézanne was somehow too trivial for him when compared with the vision of a new society, where man lives in harmony with his fellows and with nature, that he wanted his own pictures to convey.

Color as the vehicle of human emotions

Gauguin's Messianic attitude to art was shared by his one-time friend and companion, Vincent van Gogh. The son of a Dutch Protestant pastor, van Gogh was a man of passionate if unorthodox religious convictions, which he wished to communicate to others. He turned to painting only after his failure as an evangelist and a teacher. Through his pictures he preached a message of Christian love and charity, making himself the champion of the outcast and the underdog. With *The Potato Eaters* (p. 170), van Gogh, wishing like Millet before him to celebrate the simple dignity of humble peasant folk, chose to paint them partaking of a near-sacramental act.

Shortly after finishing *The Potato Eaters* van Gogh left his native Holland for Paris, and the remainder of his short life was spent in France. The heavy, somber, dark-toned way of painting that he had learned seemed inadequate now for his ambitions. He aspired to something more expressive. Color was the key to a new world. With the tremendous sense of excitement that characterizes his work, he absorbed all he could of modern painting as it had been evolved in Paris, studying Delacroix and the Impressionists, then the work of Seurat and Gauguin.

It was with Gauguin that van Gogh hoped to establish a community of painters at Arles, in the south of France. But as is well known, this was not to be. The two men were temperamentally incompatible, and their association at Arles brought into the open the latent mental disease that was van Gogh's unfortunate inheritance. Only his suicide, in July, 1890, put an end to the terrifying series of mental blackouts that darkened the last part of his life.

When sane, however, van Gogh was completely sane. In these last three years he painted the pictures that are probably more widely loved today than any other works of art. Van Gogh chose ordinary everyday things to paint. But believing that, as he said, "all reality is symbolic," he gave them a value much greater and more universal than the things themselves. His pictures are often charged with a personal significance, as in the still-lifes of empty bird's-nests done just before he left his home in Holland; or in his last work, *Crows over a Wheat Field* (p. 175), in which he seems to have painted the scene of his suicide, with menacing black crows overhead, and field-paths that do not lead away but bear down upon the artist and offer him no means of escape. In such pictures we share his emotions, identifying ourselves with his whole tragic existence in a way that is impossible with artists of earlier generations.

Van Gogh's remarkable success in transmitting his emotions resulted partly from the eloquence of the language that he fashioned for himself. No one drew, or handled paint, with quite the same nervous intensity: the dabs and strokes of van Gogh's brush communicate at once with the spectator. He was unwilling to work from memory, as Gauguin demanded that he should, but used colors for their emotional and expressive qualities with a direct power that has never been equaled. Again we have an intimation of the art that the 20th century was to bring.

The 1890's: a period of waiting

Van Gogh died in 1890, Seurat a year later; Gauguin spent most of the decade in Tahiti; Monet, Renoir and Cézanne were working quietly in the country. In consequence, the artistic atmosphere of Paris throughout the 1890's was very different from what it was in the immediately preceding decades. Of the older painters, only Degas was still in Paris, and he lived in almost complete seclusion. One of his admirers, however, will always be associated with the 1890's—Count Henri de Toulouse-Lautrec. He shared Degas' almost exclusive concern with the female figure and also his interest in movement. But although less objective and inventive

than Degas, Lautrec had a bond of sympathy with his subjects, most of whom lived like himself on the fringe of society, that Degas never possessed.

The 1890's in Paris were a decade of retrenchment, a breathing space before the next astonishing sequence of artistic discoveries, which began shortly after the turn of the century. The little group of Gauguin followers who called themselves "Nabis," the Hebrew word for prophets, was inaugurated with declarations that were indeed of prophetic tenor. Such, for example, was Maurice Denis' statement that "sounds, colors, words, have a miraculously expressive value, beyond representation and any literal meaning," or, written in 1890, his: "Remember that any painting, before being a warhorse, a nude, or some anecdote, is essentially a flat surface covered with colors arranged in a certain order."

Neither Denis nor his friends, however, were able to put their precepts into practice. Their influence was to be a more subtle and indirect one, in, for instance, the development of the ornamental decorative style eventually known as Art Nouveau. Édouard Vuillard and Pierre Bonnard were the only Nabis who proved themselves to be painters of consequence, and they returned, after the experimental work of their earliest years, to something closer to Impressionism.

Activity outside Paris

The change in the artistic temperature of Paris meant an opportunity for painters elsewhere. One feels a sudden intensification of activity in the 1890's in other European cultural centers. Ensor was working in Antwerp, Munch in Berlin, Toorop in Amsterdam, Steer and Sickert and Beardsley in London. This was the beginning of the internationalism that has characterized 20th-century art.

What had gone on in the previous forty years or so in these places can in no degree be compared with what had happened in France. In general, the best painters working outside Paris during that period were either, like Eakins and Homer, or the Dutch landscape painters, or Liebermann and Leibl, naturalists, sometimes influenced by Courbet and the Impressionists; or they were Symbolists of the more literary kind, at their best when gifted with a strongly personal vision, such as von Marées or Hodler, Rossetti or Burne-Jones, or Albert Pinkham Ryder. The most interesting and original of all was probably the American James Whistler, who made his headquarters in London in the early 1860's. Like his friend Dante Gabriel Rossetti, he experienced a dissatisfaction with naturalistic painting at least a decade before the French crisis of the 1880's. But neither painter could really see his way through to a new art of the future, though an occasional picture, such as Whistler's *Nocturne in Black and Gold: The Falling Rocket* (p. 189), does possess an extraordinary modernity.

In the second half of the 19th century it was apparently only in the artistic climate of Paris that the right conditions existed—conditions that fostered one of the most remarkable developments in the history of art, when the whole language of painting was made into a more expressive instrument for the transmission of human feelings and emotions. Courbet and Manet; Degas, Monet, and Cézanne; Seurat, Gauguin, and van Gogh: the list of names summarizes what is surely one of the greatest artistic achievements of mankind, and one that we in the 20th century cherish for its continuing relevance to our times.

Biographies

SOME BOOKS FOR FURTHER READING

J. Lemarie, *Impressionism*, Geneva, 1955.
J. Rewald, *Post-Impressionism, from van Gogh to Gauguin*,
    New York, 1956.
J. Rewald, *The History of Impressionism*, New York, 1962.

SEE ALSO UNDER THE INDIVIDUAL BIOGRAPHIES

FRÉDÉRIC BAZILLE 1841-1870

An outdoor painter who died too young to fulfill his early promise

Frédéric Bazille was born in 1841 into a wealthy and cultured family living in Montpellier in the south of France. At the Montpellier home of the art collector Alfred Bruyas, his boyish imagination was excited by two paintings by Eugène Delacroix: *Women of Algiers* and *Daniel in the Lions' Den*. When Bazille was 18 he obtained his parents' permission to study painting, but only on the condition that he read medicine at the same time. So in 1860 he began art lessons.

After two years he went to Paris and enrolled at the École des Beaux-Arts in Charles Gleyre's studio, where he met Pierre Auguste Renoir, Claude Monet, and Alfred Sisley. The four young men soon became friends and formed a group independent of the other students. With Monet, Bazille would watch, from a window, the aged Delacroix at work in his garden studio. Like Monet he was also an admirer of Édouard Manet. During Easter, 1863, all four friends made outdoor studies in the Forest of Fontainebleau. Later that year Gleyre's studio closed down.

Bazille spent the summer of 1864, while waiting for the result of an examination in medicine, at Honfleur on the Seine estuary with Monet. There he met two marine painters, Monet's friends Eugène Boudin and Johan Barthold Jongkind. In Paris again in the autumn he found that he had failed his examination. At last his parents permitted him to study painting full time. In the Forest of Fontainebleau in 1865, when Monet was in bed for some days with an injured leg, Bazille painted *Monet, after his Accident, at the Inn in Chailly*. During the following year he was working on two canvases which he submitted to the Paris Salon, *Young Girl at the Piano* and *Still-life of Fish*. As he had feared, only the still-life was accepted.

Meanwhile the influences of Courbet and Manet encouraged Bazille, Monet,

PIERRE AUGUSTE RENOIR
Portrait of Frédéric Bazille
Paris, Louvre

Summer Scene, Bathers, 1869
Cambridge, Mass., Fogg Art Mus.

The Artist's Studio in the Rue de La Condamine, 1870
Paris, Mus. de l'Impressionnisme

and Renoir to attempt a new type of subject, figure painting in the open air. In 1865 Bazille posed for Monet's life-size, unfinished *Le Déjeuner sur l'Herbe* and himself produced a study, *The Pink Dress*, in which the figure is in the shade, silhouetted against a summer evening landscape. In 1867 he achieved a successful tonal integration of figures and background in *The Artist's Family on the Terrace*, exhibited at the Salon in 1868, but later retouched and dated 1869.

Financially more secure than most of his friends, Bazille often gave them material help. He shared his Paris studio with Monet in 1865 and, when Monet was in difficulties, arranged to buy in installments his enormous *Women in the Garden*. Renoir stayed for some time at Bazille's next studio, in the Batignolles district of Paris. This spacious room was the setting of Bazille's *The Artist's Studio in the Rue de La Condamine*, 1870, which incorporated portraits of Renoir, Manet, Monet, and the writer Émile Zola. Camille Pissarro, Paul Cézanne, and sometimes Courbet, were also visitors at his successive studios. He in turn was often present at the gatherings of the *avant garde* in the Café Guerbois. He was one of the few people capable of indulging in verbal duels with the erudite and sarcastic Edgar Degas, displaying a clarity of mind and matter-of-factness that were reflected in his work.

When the Franco-Prussian war broke out in 1870, Bazille volunteered for the regiment of the Zouaves. He was killed fighting at Beaune-la-Rolande on November 28, 1870, at the age of 29.

AUBREY VINCENT BEARDSLEY 1872-1898

An original artist in the field of graphic design

Self-portrait
London, B. M.

Aubrey Vincent Beardsley was born in Brighton on the English Channel, on August 21, 1872. He grew up a consumptive, full of an intense nervous energy and aware that he would not live long. Like many delicate children he was precocious; he became a talented pianist, an avid reader, a witty, elaborate speaker, and a devotee of the theater and Wagnerian opera.

When he was 11 his family moved to London. At the age of 16 he became a draftsman in a surveyor's office, then joined an insurance company near the well-known bookshop Jones and Evans. It was Frederick Evans who got him his first commission, for five hundred illustrations to a new edition of Malory's "Morte d'Arthur." At the age of 20 Beardsley gave up his job, to devote his days to the museums and galleries and the pursuit of social contacts, and his nights to drawing. The mock-medieval, late Pre-Raphaelite style of his work in the "Morte d'Arthur" gave way to his admiration for French painting of the 18th century and for James McNeill Whistler's *Peacock Room*, which he had seen in 1891. He abandoned all interest in realistic representation to concentrate on design in two dimensions. From Greek vases he learned to mass black against white.

Attracted by his drawings, the financier of a new magazine, "The Studio," made it a condition of his supporting the publication that Beardsley should be asked to contribute to it. In 1893 Beardsley was admitted as a member of the New English Art Club and appointed theatrical cartoonist to "The Pall Mall Budget." In 1894 his work was shown with Les XX in Brussels. But it was his drawings for "The Studio" that most quickly and effectively spread his name across Europe, and with it the flat, decorative idiom that became part of the European phenomenon of Art Nouveau.

The first issue of "The Studio" appeared in April, 1893, with an article on Beardsley and his drawing *J'ai baisé ta bouche, Iokanaan.* Both provoked the public and brought Beardsley an invitation from the London publisher John Lane to illustrate the English translation of Oscar Wilde's "Salome." The resulting designs were extremely accomplished and blatantly erotic; some were rejected as unsuitable for publication.

Lane was planning a periodical intended to challenge vested interests in art and literature and invited Beardsley to contribute. The first yellow volume appeared in April, 1894. Its color and title, "The Yellow Book," were a deliberate allusion to the more sensational type of French novel bound in yellow covers. Beardsley's cover designs, frontispieces, title pages, endpapers, and posters for it were described as "neurotic delusions," "diseased, weird, macabre, and sinister." He was dropped from "The Yellow Book" in 1895, when the trial of Oscar Wilde, with whom he was associated in the public mind, became headline news.

Ill and in financial difficulties, Beardsley was saved from his predicament by Leonard Smithers, a London dealer in "curious" and erotic books who made him a salaried draftsman on his new quarterly "The Savoy." In this were published Beardsley's intricate illustrations to Alexander Pope's poem "The Rape of the Lock" and to his own burlesque tale "Under the Hill." Although "The Savoy" ceased in 1896 and Beardsley was seriously ill, he continued to work and Smithers to support him. He produced six illustrations to Théophile Gautier's novel "Mademoiselle de Maupin" and a set of initials for Ben Jonson's "Volpone." His designs, in the nature of commentaries rather than direct illustrations to any text, reflect the foibles of his own time, the *fin de siècle.* Rich, delicate, over-all patterns were by this stage substituted for the bold black and white masses employed in his earlier work.

In search of a milder climate than that of London, Beardsley traveled to Paris and the south of France. There, converted at the last to Roman Catholicism, he died in Mentone on March 16, 1898.

A. Symons Aubrey Beardsley London, 1898 and 1949
R. A. Walker The Best of Beardsley London, 1948
K. Foss Beardsley, His Fifty Best Drawings London, 1955

HIS WORKS INCLUDE

"J'ai baisé ta bouche, Iokanaan," 1893
Princeton, N. J., University Library
The Toilet of Salome
London, B. M.
A Nightpiece, 1894
London, Tate
The Battle of Beaux and Belles: from "The Rape of the Lock," 1896
Private Coll.

See also pages 236, 237

AUBREY BEARDSLEY

The Fat Woman, 1894
London, Tate

Cover Design for
"The Yellow Book," 1894
London, Tate

ARNOLD BÖCKLIN

1827–1901

Self-portrait with Death, 1872
West Berlin, Staatl. Mus.

A Swiss Symbolist painter and forerunner of Expressionism

Arnold Böcklin was born in Basel, Switzerland, on October 16, 1827. His father, a factory manager, allowed him to attend the Basel School of Design. At 18 Böcklin went to Germany, where he studied landscape painting for two years in Düsseldorf.

He was in Paris during the revolution of 1848. Thereafter, until his death in 1901 at the age of 74, he painted in Switzerland, Germany, and Italy, spending periods of several years at a time in Basel and Zurich, Weimar and Munich, Rome and Florence.

He established his reputation in 1859 in Munich, when he exhibited his *Pan in the Bullrushes*. From 1860 to 1862 he held a teaching post at the newly founded Weimar Academy. But perhaps his closest links with Germany were the painters who influenced him. As a boy he had learned to admire the work of Hans Holbein the Younger, well represented in the Basel Museum. Among his friends in Italy

Pan and Syrinx, 1854
Dresden, Gemäldegal.

War, 1896
Zurich, Kunsthaus

20

were several contemporary German artists, including Anselm Feuerbach, a painter of idealized portraits and mythological subjects, and later Hans von Marées, a figure comparable with himself in the final flowering of German Romantic painting. While staying in Rome, Böcklin also made a long and careful study of the ancient Roman murals at Pompeii.

These successive influences encouraged him to proceed from the delicacy and subtlety of the paintings contemporary with *Pan in the Bullrushes* to an extremely individual Romantic style, not untinged by classical restraint. For many years his subjects were almost exclusively mythological.

Suddenly, in Zurich between 1885 and 1892, Böcklin adopted a much more brilliant, intense coloring. He occupied his last years, having settled in Italy near Fiesole on the outskirts of Florence, in indulging the macabre side of his vision. In 1896 he produced two canvases entitled *War*, and in 1898 *The Plague*, in which his knowledge of the Isenheim altar by Grünewald is apparent. This choice of subject-matter and his use of hard, clear outlines to define areas of strong color, anticipated certain aspects of Expressionism and Surrealism of the 20th century.

HIS WORKS INCLUDE

Pan in the Bullrushes, 1857
Munich, Neue Pin.
The Gorge of the Dragon, 1870
Munich, Schackgal.
Pietà, 1873
West Berlin, Staatl. Mus.

See also page 199

PIERRE BONNARD   1867-1947

A founder member of the Nabis

Pierre Bonnard was born on October 3, 1867, the second of three children in a conventional, middle-class family. From 1885 to 1888 he studied law in Paris, but on failing his oral examination he took a job in a government office and meanwhile attended the École des Beaux-Arts. After competing unsuccessfully for the *Prix de Rome* he entered the Académie Julian and there met Édouard Vuillard, Maurice Denis, Louis Paul Henri Sérusier, and Paul Ranson, who together were to form a group calling themselves "The Nabis." In 1889 Bonnard sold a poster design (for champagne), and on the strength of this decided to become a painter. After completing his military service he took a studio with Vuillard. This became a meeting place for the Nabis and it was occasionally visited by Paul Gauguin. In 1891 the Nabis exhibited together at Le Barc de Boutteville's gallery in a show called "Impressionists and Symbolists." Bonnard also began to show regularly at the Salon des Indépendants, and in 1891 the Natanson brothers founded "La Revue Blanche," to which Bonnard was to contribute many illustrations.

Bonnard's first one-man show was held in 1896 at the Durand-Ruel gallery. It was of this that Camille Pissarro wrote to his son; "Another Symbolist has failed miserably. And one whose coming triumph was hailed by (the critic Gustave) Geffroy in 'le Journal.' All the painters worth anything, (Pierre) Puvis (de Chavannes), Degas, Renoir, and your humble servant unanimously term hideous the exhibition held at Durand's of the Symbolist named Bonnard." (Pissarro was later to revise his opinion of Bonnard.)

Bonnard's life was uneventful. He married, and moved out of Paris in 1911 to a

Self-portrait, 1938
New York, Wildenstein Inc.

At the Moulin Rouge, 1896
*Santa Barbara, Calif.,
coll. Wright Ludington*

villa near Vernon. He also began to make yearly trips to the Midi and in 1925 bought a small house at Le Cannet; he died there on January 23, 1947.

When Bonnard arrived at the Académie Julian, Sérusier was enthusiastically spreading the "teachings" of Gauguin (with whom he had worked the previous summer) among his fellow pupils. "The painter," he said, "ought not to rest until he has given birth to the child of his imagination ... begotten in a union of his mind with reality"; thus, enhanced by the imagination, colors should be vivid, outlines strong, and the artist should concentrate on the pattern-making element in painting. Although Bonnard (and with him Vuillard) never concerned himself with the theoretical side of painting to the extent of Sérusier or Denis, his works during the 1890's were clearly guided by these principles.

Among his most characteristic "Nabi" paintings were the four large panels *Children Playing with Hoops*, about 1895. The composition is boldly asymmetrical; the color areas are flat and deliberately decorative in shape, the illusion of depth being suggested by diminution of scale alone. As is clear in this work, Bonnard was particularly interested in the compositional lessons to be learned from the Japanese print (he was nicknamed by Ranson "the very Japanese Nabi"). This preoccupation with an abstract composition rather than with "realistic" modeling of forms is quite in accordance with Denis' now famous formulation that "any painting—

HIS WORKS INCLUDE

The Parade, 1890
Switzerland, Private Coll.

The Dressing Gown, about 1890
Paris, Mus. d'Art Moderne

The Checkered Blouse, 1892
Fontainebleau, coll. Charles Terrasse

Woman on a Bed, 1899
Paris, Mus. d'Art Moderne

Man and Woman, 1900
Paris, Mus. d'Art Moderne

La Loge (Gaston and
Josse Bernheim-Jeune and
their Wives) 1908
Paris, coll. Bernheim-Jeune

See also pages 180, 230

The Cup of Coffee, about 1914
London, Tate

before being a war horse, a nude, or some anecdote—is essentially a flat surface covered with colors arranged in a certain order." Bonnard was in fact much truer to this than was Denis himself, for the latter soon became absorbed in mystical religious themes at the expense of purely pictorial considerations, while Bonnard's subject matter—incidents from Parisian life in the street, in the house— remained unobtrusive. The playful humor, suggested by the composition of the screen just mentioned, is often present in his work of the 1890's. As regards color these early works are generally rather dark and subdued in tone, only occasional touches of brighter color being used to focus attention in an unexpected direction.

Standing Nude, 1908
Brussels, Mus. Royaux des B-A.

Toward the end of the 1890's the Nabi group was slowly breaking up; Sérusier elaborated a new aesthetic theory with Jan Verkade, and while Denis and Ranson were keenly interested, Bonnard together with Vuillard and Ker Xavier Roussel remained indifferent. They exhibited together for the last time at the Durand-Ruel gallery in 1899. On this occasion Pissarro remarked of Bonnard: "This young man will go far, he has a painter's eye."

Around the turn of the century Bonnard's work was changing noticeably, becoming enriched in new directions. He was beginning to use thicker paint, a stronger, wider range of colors, and more modeling in his forms, thus breaking up the flatness of colors that had characterized his earlier work. This is clearly evident in *The Bourgeois Afternoon*, 1903, one of his most ambitious works of these years. Here a large family, their cats and dogs, the surrounding garden and houses, are all presented with a new warmth and intimacy. The background, from being a neutral backdrop, has here become an important element in the pictorial composition, rich in decorative detail.

In the following years his handling became freer and his colors stronger and more brilliant while retaining—unlike the contemporary work of the Fauves—all their subtle and soft harmony. The everchanging scene of Parisian life, the Vernon landscape, the nude, and still-life provided his subject matter. The three panels entitled *Mediterranean*, which he painted for the collector Morosoff in 1911, show Bonnard's first reaction to the southern landscape with its new colors and forms.

The years 1915 to 1920 saw a temporary tightening of his draftsmanship; as he said: "to guard against myself ... against the color that bewilders you." *The Source: Kneeling Bather*, 1917, is one of several nudes painted at this time in which Bonnard concentrated on stronger formal values. Although not sharing his drawing technique, these nudes do recall something of Degas in the unusual angle from which they are viewed.

In the 1920's the rich, glowing colors regained their importance while that of drawing diminished. Thus his painting continued essentially unchanged for the rest of his life, the color only increasing in its intensity and luminosity and the composition becoming more masterly in the balancing of tones and textures. Never, however, does the freshness of his perception and his treatment of subject seem to lessen, and the late *Southern Landscape*, 1940, shows the glorious richness which Bonnard developed in color and brushwork at the end of his life.

J. Rewald Pierre Bonnard New York, 1948

The Table, 1925
London, Tate

Étaples (detail) 1888
Manchester, England, City Art Gall.

The Beach at Tourgeville (detail) 1893
London, N. G.

EUGÈNE BOUDIN

1824-1898

A painter of seascapes and a precursor of Impressionism

Eugène Boudin was born in 1824 at Honfleur, France, on the Seine estuary opposite Le Havre. The son of a pilot on the local ships, he worked for some time as a cabin boy on the steamer that crossed the estuary. When his father retired from the sea, Boudin started work in Le Havre in a stationery and picture-framing shop, where many painters came during their summer visits to the sea. Here he made the acquaintance of Thomas Couture, Constant Troyon, and other artists. His enthusiasm for painting aroused, he began to produce landscapes in the manner of Troyon's pastoral scenes. Jean François Millet visited the shop in about 1845 and advised him on his work. With this encouragement Boudin decided to go to Paris and there began his artistic studies by making numerous copies in the Louvre.

In 1850 a Le Havre society bought two of his pictures. A year later the city of Le Havre granted him, under the sponsorship of Troyon and Couture, a three-year scholarship to study in Paris. Instead of setting himself conscientiously to work at the École des Beaux-Arts, he turned to painting in the open air.

Boudin was one of the first French painters to work directly from nature. His devotion to nature and passion for exact factual statement never diminished. The young Claude Monet was deeply impressed when he met Boudin in Le Havre and was persuaded to go out sketching with him. Boudin was to say: "Everything that is painted directly on the spot has always a strength, a power, a vividness of touch that one doesn't find again in the studio." It was from him that Monet learned the importance of retaining the "first impression, which is the good one."

Gustave Courbet, too, saw some of Boudin's work, called on him, and was escorted around Le Havre. Courbet encouraged him with some success to paint in a broader, freer style. On one occasion in Le Havre they met the poet and critic Charles Baudelaire, who was so enchanted with Boudin's work that he devoted a page of his review of the 1859 Salon to an enthusiastic account of Boudin's pastel sketches.

In 1861 Boudin spent some months again in Paris, brushing in the skies and backgrounds of his friend Troyon's pictures in order to make a living. About this time he met Camille Corot. He wrote frequently to Monet, who introduced him in 1862 to Johan Barthold Jongkind. In 1868 Boudin persuaded the organizers of and international maritime exhibition in Le Havre to invite Monet, Courbet, and Édouard Manet to participate. All three, like Boudin himself, were awarded silver medals.

It was in the 1860's that Boudin found his personal style, painting innumerable scenes of the seashore and the Seine estuary, fresh in vision and subtle in color. He recorded the changes of water and sky in a range of delicate tints of gray, to be varied a little with other colors in the 1870's. He painted groups of visitors to fashionable coastal resorts of his day, in small panels that possess the same delicate spontaneity as his seascapes. His method of painting direct from nature, his power of rendering transitory atmospheric effects and, above all, his dedication in passing on his knowledge to Monet made him one of the precursors of Impressionism.

During the Franco-Prussian war of 1870-71 he took refuge in Belgium, but as soon as he could he returned to the Normandy coast. In 1874, invited probably by Monet, he exhibited with the Impressionists at their first group show. From time to time he sent large canvases to the Paris Salon. He was able to sell some work, though to a limited number of patrons. It was only later that public taste found Boudin entirely acceptable. In the last years of his life he went south, to Antibes and Villefranche, hoping for some relief from his bad health. But he soon returned to the north of France, where he died at Deauville in 1898.

B. L. Benjamin Eugène Boudin New York, 1937

HIS WORKS INCLUDE

The Jetty, Trouville, 1869
Glasgow, Art Gall.

The Port of Antwerp, 1871
Paris, Mus. de l'Impressionnisme

The Harbor at Bordeaux, 1874
Paris, Mus. de l'Impressionnisme

See also page 138

Venice, 1897
Le Havre, Mus. des B-A.

The Harbor of Trouville, about 1888
London, N. G.

ANTOINE BOURDELLE   1861-1929

Rodin's chief assistant, who later became a major sculptor in his own right

Antoine Bourdelle was born in 1861 at Montauban in the south of France, the son of a cabinet-maker. He learned drawing with the founder of the Ingres Museum at Montauban, then sculpture at the art school in Toulouse. At the age of 24 he won a scholarship to the École des Beaux-Arts in Paris, which he left after six months in order to work on his own.

The sculptors he most admired were the 17th-century Pierre Puget and, from his own century, Antoine Louis Barye and Jean Baptiste Carpeaux. He became a friend of Jules Dalou and, most important of all, the pupil and assistant of Rodin, with whom a long collaboration followed despite their basic difference of outlook. After 1905, when he stopped working for him, Bourdelle struggled to break away from Rodin's influence, his own ideals demanding more and more insistently a complete simplicity of forms. His deep anxiety over his lack of a faith drew him

Anatole France, 1919
Paris, Mus. d'Art Moderne, et al.

25

Monument to the
Dead of Montauban, 1897
Montauban

Victory, 1915
Paris, Mus. d'Art Moderne

Sir James Frazer, 1922
Paris, Mus. d'Art Moderne

Monument to Mickiewicz, 1928-29
Paris, Place d'Alma

See also page 253

The Virgin of Alsace, about 1923
Paris, Mus. Bourdelle

to the philosophical writings of Henri Bergson and the Indian Krishnamurti.

With Rodin's help, Bourdelle soon became a well-known figure. He had already begun, in 1884, to submit portrait busts fairly regularly to the Paris Salon, where his *Hannibal's First Victory* received an honorable mention in 1885. Four years later he won a medal at the Paris World Exhibition. In 1893 he was awarded the commission for a monument to commemorate of the dead of Montauban. In 1909 his *Hercules the Archer* was much acclaimed. He refused one commission, that for a monument to a General Gallifet, who had been guilty of brutality during the Paris Commune of 1871.

Once established in Paris, Bourdelle became a popular teacher, both at the Académie de la Grande Chaumière and at his own studio. There, from 1910, many prominent pupils attended his classes, so that his influence on French sculpture was considerable. By now his work was markedly stylized. Like Rodin, he learned from Greek and Gothic art, but, unlike Rodin, he spoiled what he gained from this discipline by exaggerating the pastiche and the archaism.

A significant aspect of Bourdelle's work was his interest in dance forms and movements. In 1903 the American dancer Isadora Duncan had danced at a celebration held in honor of Rodin. Bourdelle, who was present, did not fail to realize how perfectly her movements matched his aesthetic ideal. He saw her perform again in 1909. He made numerous sketches of her and wrote: "When the great Isadora danced before me, thirty years of my life looking at all the great human masterpieces became suddenly animated." Commissioned in 1910 to decorate the Paris Théâtre des Champs-Elysées, he could visualize the proposed reliefs only in terms of Isadora. Before he finished them in 1913 he had seen Nijinsky's dancing and incorporated this, too, in his design.

Bourdelle received several commissions for monuments in his last years. He was a founder and vice-president of the Paris Salon des Tuileries, and in 1924 became a commander of the Legion of Honor. He died at Le Vésinet, near Paris, in October, 1929.

SIR EDWARD COLEY BURNE-JONES   1833-1898

A Pre-Raphaelite creator of a remarkable dream-world

Edward Coley Burne-Jones was born in Birmingham, England, on August 28, 1833. It may have been his Welsh descent on his father's side that first turned his attention to the world of imagination and ideals. In 1853, desiring to enter the Church, he went to Exeter College, Oxford, to study for the ministry. William Morris was also a student there, and the two young men became friends. Together they looked at the Italian paintings in the university gallery, the engravings of Dürer, John Millais's *The Return of the Dove to the Ark*, and Dante Gabriel Rossetti's illustrations to *The Maids of Elfenmere*. This experience was the decisive factor; Burne-Jones determined to become an artist.

The most evident sources of inspiration for his early drawings and watercolors are Italian 15th-century art, Rossetti, and his own fertile predilection for pattern and detail. He met Rossetti in London in 1856 and left Oxford that Easter without taking his degree. In 1859 and 1862 he visited Italy for himself, finding much to admire, particularly in Giotto, Michelangelo, Leonardo, Botticelli, Mantegna, and the artists of the Sienese school.

In 1856 Burne-Jones produced the first of many oil paintings, some of them for large decorative schemes. His specific aim was to create and present a beautiful dream-world. Usually he drew his subject-matter from classical or medieval mythology. His is often considered the typical Pre-Raphaelite, but was in fact of a younger generation than the members of the Pre-Raphaelite Brotherhood. Moreover, he exploited only one of its aspects, the medieval-inspired romanticism of Rossetti.

Burne-Jones's predominantly linear style exerted more influence on English illustrating and design than on painting. His output was immense and various. In 1857 he made the first of a huge number of cartoons for stained glass. His designs for tapestry included five scenes from the Holy Grail legend, 1890. These, with his drawings for furniture and organs, tiles and mosaics, contributed to the evolution of the English Arts and Crafts movement and of Art Nouveau. Most of this decorative work was done for his friend William Morris's taste-reforming furnishing and stained-glass manufactory. One of his outstanding productions for Morris was the 87 designs for the Kelmscott Press edition, 1897, of Geoffrey Chaucer.

Burne-Jones' reputation has suffered as a result of worthless imitators, but he is an important figure in the European Symbolist movement. In 1877 he took part in the Grosvenor Gallery opening exhibition, at which some of Whistler's work was also hung. He was made an associate of the Royal Academy in 1885, but resigned shortly afterwards, and a baronet in 1894. He died on June 17, 1898, after an attack of influenza.

HIS WORKS INCLUDE
Sidonia von Bork, 1560, 1860
London, Tate
Cupid's Hunting Ground
London, V. and A.
Danaë, 1872
Glasgow, Art Gall.
The Mill, 1870-72
London, V. and A.
The Golden Stairs, 1880
London, Tate
King Cophetua and the Beggar Maid 1884
London, Tate
St. George and the Dragon, about 1892
Hartford, Conn., Wadsworth Atheneum

See also page 197

Sidonia von Bork, 1560, 1860
London, Tate

"Here Lies Hoarded Love": from the Briar Rose Series, 1871-90
Buscot Park, Berkshire, England, coll. Lord Farington

A friend of Degas who helped to bring Impressionism to the United States

Mary Cassatt was born in Pittsburgh, Pennsylvania, in 1844, the daughter of a wealthy American banker. She attended the Pennsylvania Academy, then traveled in Europe, visiting France, Italy, Spain, and Holland in order to study the old masters. Finally, in 1872, she settled in Paris. She began to admire the work of Edgar Degas; he in turn noticed a painting of hers at the Paris Salon of 1874. They had not yet met, but already had in common a preference for drawing over color.

Mary Cassatt had gone to Paris intending to study with the academician Charles Chaplin. The conventional methods of painting were contrary to her independent temperament, however, and she felt an increasing desire to free herself from them. She lost interest in the Salon when a portrait of hers, rejected by the Salon jury in 1875, was accepted the next year after the background had been darkened so as to conform to academic taste.

In 1877 she was introduced to Degas, who invited her to exhibit in the Impressionist group shows. Delighted, she did so regularly, devoting herself thereafter to a type of painting that she felt to be the genuine expression of her interests. There were many studies of contemporary life, children, interiors, and gardens. When Degas refused to take part in the seventh Impressionist exhibition in 1882, Mary Cassatt followed his example. A close friendship grew up between the two, helped no doubt by their common social background and similar intellectual tastes.

She posed for several of Degas's pictures, notably *At the Milliner's*, 1882. She

At the Opera, about 1880
Boston, Mass., Mus. of Fine Arts

The Little Sisters, 1885
Glasgow, Art Gall.

A Young Woman Sewing, about 1886
Paris, Mus. de l'Impressionnisme

herself was certainly influenced by him. Her subject-matter to some extent followed his. In common with him and many of the Impressionists, however, she derived her style, especially that of her graphic work, partly from Japanese woodcuts. She was never Degas' formal pupil, however. Her work had individual qualities of line and feeling.

Mary Cassatt tried unceasingly to interest her American countrymen in Impressionism, buying pictures for herself, her family, and her friends. She attempted to help the dealer Durand-Ruel by lending him money. From 1912 she suffered, like Degas, from gradual loss of sight. On June 14, 1926, she died in the Château Beaufresne near Beauvais, France.

PAUL CÉZANNE   1839-1906

The greatest innovator in the art of the 19th century

Paul Cézanne was born in Aix-en-Provence, France, on January 19, 1839. His father, a hat dealer and probably of Italian origin, prospered after buying the local bank in 1848. Cézanne, a moody, temperamental boy, was sent to the *lycée* in Aix. There he met Émile Zola, his friend for many years. With a third boy, Baptistin Baille, they went for long walks together in the country, held lengthy discussions on their mutual interest in the arts, and wrote poetry. When Zola went to Paris with his mother in 1858, he and Cézanne continued their discussions in regular letters.

It was not until 1860 that Cézanne decided to become a painter. He made clumsy copies of works in the Aix Museum and painted a fishing scene at sunset on the wall of the drawing room at the Jas de Bouffan, his father's recently acquired house on the outskirts of Aix. His father had forced him to study law at the university of Aix, but he had enrolled at the same time at the drawing academy, where he copied plaster casts and drew from life. As he spent less and less time at his books, and more and more at painting, both in class and out-of-doors, his father eventually relented and allowed him, at the age of 22, to go to Paris to study art.

In Paris, Cézanne spent five hours every morning, from six to eleven, at the Atelier Suisse, and much of the rest of his time at the Louvre. But except for Camille Pissarro, the young painters at the atelier found his powerful, uncompromising drawings ridiculous. He was soon depressed. After only about six months, and in spite of Zola's entreaties to the contrary, he returned to Aix and worked in his father's office.

A year later, at the end of 1862, Cézanne was back in Paris at the Atelier Suisse. He lived much as before. His Sundays were spent with Zola. Through Pissarro he met Claude Monet, Frédéric Bazille, and Pierre Auguste Renoir, and would occasionally join them at the Café Guerbois. But he never indulged in argument. If there was disagreement over anything he said, he would leave immediately. In 1863 he was profoundly impressed by *Le Déjeuner sur l'Herbe* of Édouard Manet, who complimented Cézanne three years later on his still-lifes.

Self-portrait, about 1879
London, Tate

P. Cézanne

Cézanne's work, though uneven in quality, was bolder than that of either Manet or Monet. It was modeled for some time on Eugène Delacroix, Gustave Courbet, Honoré Daumier, and Spanish masters like Francisco de Zurbarán and José Ribera. On long stays in Aix in 1865 and 1866, Cézanne painted his portraits of his uncle, his father, and the painter Achille Emperaire in a heavy, palette-knife technique and dark colors. In the later 1860's his subject matter was highly imaginative and full of erotic fantasy. His paintings were difficult to sell. The dealer Père Martin took occasional canvases, but they did not fetch good prices. One painting, which Cézanne showed in a shop window in Marseilles, so infuriated the crowd who saw it that it had to be withdrawn.

Unlike Manet, Cézanne felt the greatest contempt for every kind of official art. He had exhibited work in 1863 at the Salon des Réfusés, but it seems to have given him considerable pleasure to be rejected the next year at the Salon proper, to which he annually made a point of sending his most "difficult" paintings. Even the energetic and authoritative support of the landscape painter Daubigny failed to prevent his *Portrait of Valabrèque* from being rejected in 1866. But when Cézanne realized that his work was being regularly, apparently almost automatically, refused at the Salon, he wrote to its Director of Fine Arts to protest, demanding a second Salon des Réfusés. The letter was not answered.

At the same time, the slow progress he believed himself to be making kept Cézanne in a constant state of depression. When the Franco-Prussian war began in 1870, he returned to the south of France to avoid conscription. Living in L'Estaque outside Marseilles with the model Hortense Fiquet, who later became his wife, he painted landscapes of remarkable expressive power. But in 1872 he deliberately set out to change his style, and went to live at Auvers-sur-Oise to be near Pissarro. He wanted to learn the new Impressionist way of painting, with its small brushstrokes, broken colors, and convincing observation of the fall of light.

The Negro Scipio, about 1868
São Paolo, Mus. and Art Gall.

An Old Man, about 1868
Paris, Louvre

The House of Père Lacroix, Auvers, 1873
Washington, D.C., N.G., Chester Dale Coll.

He even copied one of Pissarro's paintings and then began a series of landscapes which, in their turn, influenced the older man. Pissarro was, with Monet, active in organizing an exhibition of work by painters unacceptable at the official Salon. It was at his insistence that Cézanne was included in the first Impressionist group show of 1874.

One of Cézanne's exhibits on this occasion was *A Modern Olympia*, received by the public with shocked amusement. The 16 works that he contributed to the third group show in 1877 fared no better, and those that he submitted to the Salon jury each year were as regularly rejected as before. He was already in continual financial distress when his father discovered the liaison with Hortense Fiquet and reduced his allowance; his mother had then to advance him money in secret.

There were other sources of help on which Cézanne was able to draw, however. In Auvers-sur-Oise he painted some still-lifes in the house of Dr. Gachet, an *habitué* of the Café Guerbois, who lent him an etching press and bought some of his work. He was introduced by Pissarro to the Paris paint seller and art dealer Père Tanguy, who took some of his pictures in exchange for paints and canvas. Renoir introduced him to the collector Victor Chocquet, who bought one picture and asked Cézanne to paint his portrait. Cézanne's friend Zola also helped him with money on several occasions, and welcomed him at his house at Médan, on the Seine, during the summer. But in 1886 Zola published his novel "L'Oeuvre," which was about an unsuccessful artist. Cézanne, deeply hurt by the interpretation of his own work implicit in it, broke off all connection with him.

The death of his father in October, 1886 left Cézanne no longer in want. His marriage with Hortense had taken place only a few months before, after he had ceased to love her. Apart from long, frequent visits to Paris, he now lived with his mother at the Jas de Bouffan. However, when his mother died in 1897, the Jas de Bouffan was sold. Cézanne, afflicted from 1890 with diabetes and growing more and more irritable and difficult, continued to work in and around Aix. In 1901 he

Man with a Pipe, about 1892
London, Courtauld Inst. Gall.

Aix, Rocky Landscape, about 1887
London, N. G.

Still-life with a Fruit Basket, about 1890
Paris, Mus. de l'Impressionnisme

An Old Woman with a Rosary,
about 1898
London, N. G.

had a studio near Aix and in his last years he seldom left the south of France. While painting near the studio on October 15, 1906, he was caught in a storm, soaked to the skin, and had to be carried home. He collapsed while out painting the next day, and died on October 22.

In the last 20 years of his life, Cézanne traveled a long way from Impressionism. Bent on conveying in his canvases the essential structure that lay behind each appearance, he evolved a solid, analytical, extremely personal style, closer in intention to that of painters like Paul Gauguin and Vincent van Gogh than to any form of Impressionism. In 1890 he began the famous sequence of card players, but his specific aim was to "do Poussin again in contact with nature," and it was to this end that he painted innumerable views of the country around Aix: the Mont Sainte-Victoire, the forest, the Bibémus quarry. Only gradually becoming aware of his own genius, he set himself such a high standard that he could not help but fall far short of it. Yet his technique acquired a new assurance. With the great series of bathers he created a pastoral idyll suggested, possibly, by memories of his youth. He also took up watercolor, and achieved an extraordinary brilliance and luminosity in the medium.

In the early 1880's, quite unknown to Cézanne, a group of painters of a younger generation saw and admired his work at Père Tanguy's. After the publication of a short article on him by the writer J. K. Huysmans, his name occurred from time to time in various Symbolist periodicals. In 1889 Victor Chocquet arranged for *The House of the Hanged Man at Auvers-sur-Oise* to be shown at the Paris World Exhibition. Cézanne was also invited, and finally consented, to exhibit in Brussels with Les XX. A one-man show held for him in Paris in 1895 by the dealer Vollard amazed and excited younger painters and collectors, and this rapidly growing reputation was confirmed at later exhibitions, especially the retrospective one at the Salon d'Automne of 1907. It was Cézanne who opened the way for several of the most important movements of modern art, including Futurism and, above all, Cubism.

M. Schapiro Cézanne New York, 1939
P. Cézanne Letters London, 1941
E. Loran Cézanne's Composition Los Angeles, 1943
J. Rewald Cézanne London, 1948

LOVIS CORINTH   1858-1925

A German realist and expressionist painter

Lovis Corinth was born on July 21, 1858, at Tapiau in eastern Prussia. As a child he sought relief from his hostile brothers and sisters by drawing. His ability was noticed by his father, a master tanner, who sent him to study art in Königsberg (now Kaliningrad) on the Baltic.

At the age of 20, Corinth went to the Munich Academy, and at 26 to Paris, where he took lessons at the Académie Julian and painted mostly portraits. He was unmoved by what he saw of Impressionism in Paris, but admired the realism of a painting by Wilhelm Leibl, *The Poachers*, that was on view there. Corinth's stylistic masters at this time were Rembrandt, Rubens, Frans Hals, Velázquez, and the realist *par excellence*, Gustave Courbet. When Corinth was in Paris more than 20 years later, he went daily to the Louvre.

He left Paris in 1887, lived for a short time in Berlin, and then, apart from frequent journeys in Germany, Switzerland, and Denmark, he settled in Munich until 1900. The gay life he enjoyed in Berlin was mirrored in the work he did there, which grew richer and brighter as he laid on his pigments more thickly and freely. He opened an art school, and later married one of his first pupils. With Max Liebermann he became one of the leaders of German Impressionism, though his vision remained closer to that of Rembrandt than to that of any of the French Impressionists. When he visited Holland in the early years of the 20th century, he still sought out and studied the work of Rembrandt and Hals.

Corinth was partly incapacited by a stroke in 1911, but quickly recovered and in 1919 he built a house on the Walchensee, the scene of much of his later work. His style became much looser during his last years, and in about 1916 his color, in paintings now expressionist in feeling, became brighter and richer. A few months before his death in July, 1925, in Holland, he wrote: "I have discovered something new: true art is the representation of the unreal."

Corinth won recognition first in France, then in Germany. He showed at the Paris Salon in 1884 and won an honorable mention there six years later. In 1911 he was elected chairman and in 1915 president of the Berlin Sezession, where his 60th birthday was celebrated in 1918. He was awarded the freedom of his birthplace, Tapiau; an honorary doctorate at the university of Königsberg, where there was a large Corinth exhibition the year before he died; and honorary membership of the Munich Academy.

Donna Gravida
(Portrait of Charlotte Behrend) 1909
West Berlin, Staatl. Mus.

HIS WORKS INCLUDE

The Temptation of St. Anthony, 1897
Munich, Neue Pin.

Portrait of Gerhart Hauptmann, 1900
Mannheim, Kunsthalle

Emperor's Day in Hamburg, 1911
Cologne, Wallraf-Richartz-Mus.

Cowshed, 1922
Amsterdam, Stedelijk Mus.

Ecce Homo, 1925
Basel, Kunstmuseum

See also page 208

The Rumpf Family, 1901
West Berlin, Staatl. Mus.

The Trojan Horse, 1924
West Berlin, Staatl. Mus.

33

Gustave Courbet

G. Courbet.

GUSTAVE COURBET

The leading practitioner of realist painting

Gustave Courbet was born at Ornans near Besançon, France, on June 10, 1819, of partly peasant stock. His character, influenced from the first by his grandfather's strong republican feelings, was a singularly aggressive one. He was violently anti-clerical, disliked book-learning, and was interested only in painting and drawing. He studied in Besançon with a disciple of Jacques Louis David, who taught him to fill his sketchbooks with portraits and details of street scenes. His early landscapes and portraits were among his most successful works.

After arguments with his parents Courbet went to Paris, where he lived frugally and worked hard. He was not interested in academic institutions and instead attended the Atelier Suisse, where for a small fee clients could draw or paint the model in whatever way they wished. Courbet began to paint with a palette-knife in addition to his brushes.

He spent several years in Paris and Ornans. From 1844 he exhibited regularly at the Paris Salon. Some of the critics reviewed his works favorably and his name became known to a substantial public. In 1847 he visited Holland, admiring the Dutch painters, especially Rembrandt. He was influenced, in particular, by 17th-century realism in Dutch, French, and Spanish painting.

The year 1848 was one of revolutions in Europe. In France King Louis Philippe was forced to abdicate. Courbet was horrified at the repression and slaughter that followed. Spurred on by his friendship with the socialist writer Pierre Joseph Proud'hon he assumed the part of politician and social philosopher. He began to frequent the Andler Keller *brasserie* and the Brasserie des Martyrs in Paris, where he held a sort of court, airing his opinions on all subjects to *habitués* who included Camille Corot, Honoré Daumier, and the poet and critic Charles Baudelaire.

After Dinner at Ornans, 1849
Lille, Pal. des B-A.

The Burial at Ornans, 1849
Paris, Louvre

His art could not remain untouched by his politics. Between 1848 and 1850 he painted four of his largest and most important works: *After Dinner at Ornans*, *The Stone Breakers*, *The Burial at Ornans*, and *Return from the Fair*. It was usual at that time for *genre* paintings to be small. Courbet shattered all precedent by making the figures almost life size. In *The Burial at Ornans* there are more than 40 such figures, realistic portraits of various members of the Ornans community, somber in color and arranged like a frieze. *After Dinner at Ornans* was shown at the Salon of 1849 and eventually purchased by the French government. In 1850 Courbet exhibited *The Burial at Ornans*, *The Stone Breakers*, and several landscapes in Besançon, where they were admired, and in Dijon, where they aroused political turmoil.

One canvas summed up Courbet's somewhat confused theories of realism. This was *The Painter's Studio*, 1855, an intended allegory of contemporary life. Feeling strongly that a painter should only paint what he can actually see, Courbet here represented himself in his Paris studio among art collectors, members of the various social classes, and his friends. When the authorities of the 1855 Paris World Exhibition refused *The Painter's Studio*, he organized a private display of his work and called it the Pavilion of Realism.

Courbet sometimes painted landscapes out-of-doors, though he finished them

The Trellis, 1863
Toledo, Ohio, Mus. of Art

Portrait of Jo
(La Belle Irlandaise) 1865
Kansas City, Mo., William Rockhill Nelson
Gall. of Art

indoors. Certainly his figures were added in the studio. In 1854 he visited the art collector Alfred Bruyas in Montpellier and encountered the color and light of the south of France. His palette was soon brighter and more luminous than it had been. *The Winnowers* of 1854, like Courbet's boldest composition, *The Bride's Toilet*, 1865-70, contains a hint of a new conception of perspective based on actual appearance rather than on a geometrical, Renaissance system. This innovation was developed later by Paul Cézanne.

In 1863, Courbet's anticlerical *Return from the Conference* was rejected at the Salon des Réfusés as well as at the official Salon. Finally it was bought and destroyed by an indignant churchman. In the mid-1860's, however, Courbet became fashionable. His range of subject matter was wide and varied. Landscapes, portraits, still-lifes, animals in the snow, and hunting scenes were all treated with vitality and directness. He also painted nude compositions of a smoother type.

The last years of his life were disturbed ones. During the Paris Commune of 1871, having recently refused the Legion of Honor, he was named president of a committee formed to preserve works of art. He was also involved in the demolition of Napoleon's column in the Place Vendôme, and upon the collapse of the Commune he was tried and imprisoned for this offense. In 1873 he was ordered to pay for the reconstruction of the column. He fled to Switzerland, where he died near Vevey in 1877. Soon afterwards the French government sold the contents of his Paris studio.

Courbet's role in the history of painting is twofold. On the one hand he continued and matured the European realist tradition. On the other, it was his preoccupation not with the subject, but with the pictorial means, that made Impressionism possible. Even the Cubists regarded him as the father of modern painting.

M. Zahar   Gustave Courbet   London, 1951
G. Mack   Gustave Courbet   London and New York, 1952

La Grotte de la Loup, 1865
Washington, D. C., N. G., Gift of Charles L. Lindemann

Still-life: Apples and Pomegranate, 1871
London, N. G.

JULES DALOU

1838-1902

HIS WORKS INCLUDE
Alphonse Legros, about 1876
London, Tate
Charity, 1877
London, Tate
Studies for the Monument to the
Working Class, 1889-1902
Paris, Petit-Palais
Monument to Delacroix, 1890
Paris, Luxembourg Gardens

See also page 246

A successful French sculptor who was a contemporary of Rodin

Jules Dalou was born in Paris in 1838. At the age of 14 he entered the Petite École, where he was a contemporary of Auguste Rodin. From the age of 16 he studied at the École des Beaux-Arts under Francisque Joseph Duret and Albe de Poujol. He was at this time influenced by the various styles, both classical and Baroque, of François Girardon, Antoine Coysevox, and other French sculptors of the late 17th and early 18th centuries. His own style, when it consolidated, was, however, realistic.

After being implicated in the Paris Commune in 1871, Dalou's left-wing convictions forced him to take refuge in London. From 1872 until he returned to France in 1879, Dalou exhibited with the Royal Academy in London. He found patrons among the English aristocracy and was appointed to the staff of the City and Guilds Art School. He became friendly with the French-born painter, etcher, and teacher, Alphonse Legros, of whom he made a portrait sculpture. Legros helped him to obtain a teaching post at the Royal College of Art, from which he held sway over the development of English sculpture. Alfred Gilbert, the sculptor of *Eros* in Piccadilly Circus, was one of his pupils.

While in England, Dalou produced an interesting series of terracotta statuettes

Two Butchers
Paris, Petit-Palais

Charity: Study for a Group in the
Fountain behind the Royal
Exchange, London, about 1877
Birmingham, England, City Art Gall.

Le Terrassier
Paris, Petit-Palais

37

and groups. In 1877 he was given the commission for a marble group entitled *Charity*, to stand over a drinking fountain near the Royal Exchange in London. Although he finished this in the summer of the same year, it was not put into place until 1879. But perhaps his most celebrated, certainly his most copied, sculpture was *The French Peasant Woman*, first exhibited at the Royal Academy in 1873.

Back in France in 1879, Dalou executed a number of public monuments and busts. The vast *Triumph of the Republic*, 1879-99, and *The Procession of Silenus*, 1885, were set up in Paris in the Luxembourg Gardens. During the latter part of his career Dalou's earlier realism was modified toward the Baroque in which he had always been interested. He was a prizewinner at the Paris World Exhibition of 1889 and became an officer of the Legion of Honor in the same year. He was also a founder of the Société Nationale des Beaux-Arts and the first president of its sculpture section. He died in Paris in 1902, leaving unfinished a grandiose design for a *Monument to the Working Class*.

Monument to Eugène Delacroix, 1890
Paris, Luxembourg Gardens

Study for the Monument to the Working Class: Labor in the Fields
Paris, Petit-Palais

HONORÉ DAUMIER   1808-1879

A satirical painter, lithographer, and sculptor of extraordinary boldness and freedom

Honoré Daumier was born in Marseilles, France, on February 26, 1808. His father, a glazier and frame maker of poetic aspirations, took his family in 1816 to Paris, where Daumier was to spend most of his life. He worked as an office boy, then as a bookseller's clerk, but his only interest was drawing. In 1822, at the age of 14, he was allowed to attend the Atelier Suisse. There he met the future sculptor Auguste Préault, whose modeling later impressed him.

At the age of 17, Daumier became a studio assistant to the printer Zéphirin Félix Belliard, emerging after a few years with a thorough training in lithography. But when he began to produce brilliant cartoons for the radical papers, he found himself in trouble. In 1832 he was fined and put in prison for six months for caricaturing King Louis Philippe as Rabelais's Gargantua. After his release he continued in the same vein, beginning his *Illustrations of the Parliamentary Bourgeoisie* and publishing the *Rue Transnonain at 4 a.m. on April 13, 1834*, a commemoration of a disgraceful panic on the part of government troops in Paris, in which innocent people were massacred.

In August, 1835, the press was muzzled by the French government. "La Caricature," a paper for which Daumier worked, was suppressed, while "Le Char-ivari," another publication to which he contributed, was forced to abandon political satire and be content with ridiculing the bourgeois society.

Daumier then created the figure of Robert Macaire, the embodiment of society in the virulent cartoons with which he finally established his reputation. This success made it only more difficult for Daumier to appear in the public mind as a serious artist. Between 1835 and 1845 he published a vast number of lithographs, leaving himself scarcely any time for painting.

In 1848 King Louis Philippe was deposed. The short-lived Second Republic put the management of artistic affairs suddenly into more liberal hands. Everything that was submitted to the Paris Salon was hung. Daumier was persuaded by Gustave Courbet to enter a competition for a figure symbolizing the new republic. He was chosen one of the finalists, but found himself unable to produce a finished picture. Nevertheless he embarked upon a painting of an episode in the revolution. In 1849 he was given a state commission for a religious picture intended for a provincial church, but the work was not forthcoming. In 1863, after 14 years of waiting, the ministry accepted his *Drunkenness of Silenus* in its place.

Neither his large painting *The Miller, His Son, and the Ass*, nor his work *Nymphs Pursued by Satyrs*, shown at the Paris Salons of 1849 and 1850 respectively, was popular with contemporary critics. He did not exhibit at the Salon after 1853. His

The Miller, His Son, and the Ass, 1849
Glasgow, Art Gall., Burrell Coll.

The Good Bottle
Stockholm, Nationalmus.

The Butcher, about 1857
Cambridge, Mass., Fogg Art Mus.

spontaneous, sketchy style, admired in the 20th century by Pablo Picasso, was far in advance of his time and appreciated only by a few of his fellow painters, among them Eugène Delacroix and later Paul Cézanne.

Daumier knew Delacroix, Jean Baptiste Corot, Courbet, Jean François Millet, and the sculptor Antoine Louis Barye. Millet, with whom he shared an admiration for Michelangelo, influenced both his style and his subject matter. Daumier also borrowed certain motifs, such as the long lines of figures spread out across the canvas of the *Refugees*, or the theme of the artist with art collectors, from the academic painter Ernest Meissonier.

In order to have time to paint, Daumier had neglected his lithographic work. In 1860 he was dismissed from "Le Charivari." In the next four years, before he returned to the paper in 1864, he probably produced the bulk of his painting, small-scale scenes of everyday life—working types, children playing, railroad passengers, artists, and collectors—executed both in oils and watercolor. Among his few works of sculpture one of the most expressive is the figure of Ratapoil, who represented all the ignominy and vice of the society into which Daumier was born. There is also a bas-relief of about 1851 on the subject of refugees.

In 1868 Daumier left for Valmondois. He was still tied to the never-ending production of lithographs in order to make a living, but his later paintings, mainly of Don Quixote and Sancho Panza, were unique in their freedom of handling. In 1873, still in poverty, he began to go blind. Corot gave him the house at Valmondois in which he had settled, and eventually the French government granted him a pension. A large Daumier exhibition was held in Paris in 1878 by the dealer Durand-Ruel. In February of the following year Daumier died at Valmondois.

J. Lassaigne Daumier London, 1957
K. E. Maison Daumier Drawings London and New York, 1960

An Artist in his Studio
Reims, Mus. des B-A.

The Print Collector
Paris, Petit-Palais

Pierrot Strumming his Guitar, 1868
Winterthur, Switzerland, coll. Oscar Reinhart

EDGAR DEGAS   1834-1917

An artist who blended tradition with a great inventiveness of design

Edgar Degas was born into a wealthy family in Paris in 1834. His parents intended him to take up law, but late in 1855 he abandoned this idea and became instead an erratic pupil of the academic painter Louis Lamothe at the Paris École des Beaux-Arts. Lamothe had been a pupil of Jean Auguste Dominique Ingres, whom Degas admired and had indeed met. Degas never entirely rejected the Ingres tradition and never forgot his advice to "draw lines." He also admired Eugène Delacroix and Gustave Courbet.

From 1856 he traveled in Italy, to Florence, Rome, and Naples, making a series of drawings after old masters. In Florence in 1859 he painted an unusual portrait composition of the Bellelli family, his cousins.

Inspired by the writings on art of the brothers Goncourt, Degas devised for himself a new program of subject-matter. There were some things that he was never to depict; the others, which included cafés at night and dancers, occupied him for the rest of his life. As to style, like many contemporary painters he absorbed the graphic qualities, the sensitive line, and the unconventional compositions of Japanese prints. In the Louvre he copied the Italian Primitives, and Hans Holbein, Nicolas Poussin, and Delacroix.

Édouard Manet met him in the Louvre; a common background and a similar attitude of mind made them friends. But Degas was of a solitary disposition. At the Café Guerbois in Paris, where the Impressionists and their friends met for discussion, he was often involved in arguments, in which his ready erudition and frequent sarcasm allowed few of the others to compete with him.

During 1860 Degas painted *The Young Spartans Exercising*, a classical subject with the girls and boys of contemporary Montmartre for models. In the next few years

The Orchestra of the Paris Opera, about 1869
Paris, Mus. de l'Impressionnisme

The Cotton Exchange, New Orleans, 1872
Pau, Mus. des B-A.

False Start, about 1871
New York, coll. Mr. and Mrs. John Hay Whitney

41

The Café Singer Wearing a Glove
1878
Cambridge, Mass., Fogg Art Mus.

he exhibited several canvases at the Paris Salon and won praise from Pierre Puvis de Chavannes and the critic Castagnary. After the Franco-Prussian war of 1870-71, which he spent in the infantry, he started to paint the dancers of the Opera, making innumerable sketches during their ballet classes. *The Dancing Class*, 1874, is one of many compositions on the theme.

In 1872 Degas went to the United States with his brother to visit relatives in New Orleans. But although he was fascinated by the new and colorful life, he found it difficult to assimilate and did only a little painting: his uncle's cotton exchange in New Orleans and a portrait of his cousin Mme. René de Gas. In 1870 and 1873 he visited Italy again. Afterwards he went south periodically, several times to Spain and, in 1889, to Morocco.

The first group exhibition of the Impressionists, for which the photographer Nadar lent his vacant studios, was held in Paris in 1874. Degas, hoping to lessen its revolutionary nature, was insistent that as many artists as possible should participate, though he was unable to persuade Manet to do so. In 1877 he was introduced to the American painter Mary Cassatt, whose work he had noticed at the Salon three years before, and a long friendship began. He invited her to show with the Impressionists in 1879. Although the group shows were usually received by the public with hostility and ridicule, Degas exhibited in all eight except that of 1882, when he abstained as a protest against the exclusion of his followers. He felt scorn for those of the Impressionists group who, like Claude Monet, were occasionally driven by lack of funds to try to exhibit at the Salon. He himself had submitted nothing to the Salon since 1870. It was only when he gave up part of his fortune to help his brother that he had sometimes to sell his work. He hated to part with any of his paintings, to which he would often return for small alterations.

During the 1870's Degas had begun to sketch in *cafés concerts* and circuses,

A Ballet Dancer
London, Tate, et al.

A Woman Combing her Hair (detail) 1880-85
Paris, Mus. de l'Impressionnisme

recording the life of Paris with complete detachment. At the Café de la Nouvelle-Athènes, which was the setting in 1876 for his painting *The Absinthe Drinker*, a table was always reserved for him and his friends.

He produced a series of compositions of women at their toilet—bathing, drying themselves, or combing their hair. He experimented with various mediums, including watercolor, pastel with oil, etching, lithography, and monotype; he was also an active sculptor. To the sixth Impressionist group show, in 1881, he contributed a wax statuette of a young dancer, modeled with great realism and dressed in a muslin tutu, with a bow tied around the hair.

In 1885 Degas met Paul Gauguin, whom he helped on several occasions. He liked Gauguin's work. When it was auctioned in 1891, he bought a painting and began to form an art collection. In 1885, too, he met Walter Sickert, through whom his influence reached English painting. His work was shown several times at the New English Art Club in London. In 1886 the dealer Durand-Ruel took some of his pictures to New York. They had a varied reception. Degas was also asked to exhibit with Les XX, but declined the invitation.

In his later years, when his eyesight was failing, he worked almost exclusively in pastels, wax, or clay. His color glowed more than it had and his forms became broader and richer, almost dissolving into the strokes and hatchings. Degas spent these years in isolation, growing more and more disillusioned with his own work. He stopped attending the Impressionist dinners held in Paris every month. At the very last, unable to work and virtually blind, he wandered the Paris streets.

J. Rewald Degas: Works in Sculpture New York and London, 1957
P. Cabanne Degas London, 1958

A Woman Sponging her Foot
Paris, Mus. de l'Impressionisme

HIS WORKS INCLUDE

Madame Camus, 1870
Washington, D. C., N. G.

The Absinthe Drinker, 1876
Paris, Mus. de l'Impressionnisme

La La at the Cirque Fernando, Paris, about 1879
London, N. G.

Portrait of Charles Duranty, 1879
Glasgow, Art Gall.

At the Milliner's, 1882
New York, Met. Mus.

Woman Drying her Neck, 1898
Paris, Mus. de l'Impressionnisme

See also pages 134, 135, 136, 137, 215, 219, 248, 249

Women Ironing (detail) 1884
Paris, Mus. de l'Impressionnisme

A Ballet Dancer
London, Tate, et al.

The Gross Clinic, 1875
Philadelphia, Pa., Jefferson Medical College

HIS WORKS INCLUDE

The Chess Players, 1876
New York, Met. Mus.

The Pathetic Song, 1881
Washington, D. C., Corcoran Gall.

The Writing Master, 1882
New York, Met. Mus.

Portrait of
Letitia Wilson Jordan Bacon, 1888
New York, Brooklyn Mus.

Portrait of
Professor Henry A. Rowland, 1891
Andover, Mass., Addison Gall.

See also page 186

Portrait of Miss van Buren, about 1891
Washington, D. C., Phillips Coll.

THOMAS EAKINS   1844-1916

An American realist painter and revolutionary teacher of art

Thomas Eakins was born in Philadelphia on July 25, 1844. There he studied art at the Pennsylvania Academy, and also anatomy at the Jefferson Medical College. His interest in the scientific approach to art persisted, to reappear later in several paintings and in the stress he laid, as a teacher, on the mastery of anatomy.

Eakins went to Paris in 1866, spending three years under Jean Léon Gérôme and a short time with Léon Bonnat at the École des Beaux-Arts. A journey to Spain in 1870 was equally important in his development. The paintings of Velázquez and Ribera, like those of Rembrandt, remained his permanent favorites. Édouard Manet had recently been impressed in much the same way by Spanish art.

In July, 1870, Eakins returned to Philadelphia, where he stayed for the rest of his life. Fairly frequent exhibitions of his thorough, penetrating paintings of local scenes and local people made him well known but by no means popular. He needed his private income to supplement poor sales. Not only were his ideas too progressive for the Philadelphia community, but he also lacked the necessary tact to impose them successfully.

As a teacher he was remarkable. He started with a post at the Pennsylvania Academy in 1876 and became principal three years later. He was then able to reform the curriculum, with improvements that reflected his Paris training. Under his rule the pupils studied the living figure in detail, with emphasis on anatomy and even dissection. They were also encouraged to begin by learning to paint rather than to draw. The inhabitants of Philadelphia, however, did not approve of the study of the nude. Pressure was brought to bear on Eakins. He resigned in 1886, but many elements of his teaching remained. Some of them, such as modeling in clay or drawing with a brush, were assimilated by his assistant Thomas Anshutz. Eakins taught for some years at the Art Students League of Philadelphia, started a school of his own, and lectured in anatomy at various other schools.

His work meanwhile developed and matured. Two of the most outstanding paintings are *The Gross Clinic*, 1875, and *The Agnew Clinic*, 1889, both of which caused an uproar among critics and public. Their subject matter and treatment are Rembrandtesque, the approach stark and factual. The life-size figures make a tremendous impact on the spectator. Prejudice, however, prevented *The Gross Clinic* from being shown in the American section of the International Centennial Exhibition held in Philadelphia in 1876. In the mid-1880's Eakins turned mainly to portraiture, though his realism still barred him from any commercial success and his sitters were mostly his friends. Later his work lost its impetus and its vigor.

Eakins's large oeuvre was one of the first to be created out of American everyday life. It embodied a realism strong in plastic feeling and awareness of light, in vitality and psychological insight.

L. Goodrich   *Thomas Eakins, his Life and Work*   New York, *1933*
F. Porter   *Thomas Eakins*   New York, *1959*

JAMES ENSOR 1860-1949

A Belgian painter of macabre imagination

James Ensor was born on April 13, 1860, in Ostend, Belgium. His mother was Belgian, his father an English expatriate. The family's only source of income was a souvenir shop kept by Mme. Ensor on the rue de Flandre in Ostend. Here she sold puppets, fans, china, objects made of seashells, and carnival masks—bric-à-brac that was to appear in startling guises in Ensor's work.

Ensor had only two years of formal schooling, begun when he was 13. At a very early age, however, he started drawing and painting the countryside around Ostend. He took lessons from two local watercolorists and, aged 17, entered the Brussels Academy. During his three years as a student there he achieved a direct, simple, somber style, influenced to some extent by the French Impressionists and to a large degree by his own sensuous appreciation of textures. He laid on his paint frequently with a palette-knife rather than a brush.

In 1880 Ensor returned to Ostend, where he lived for the rest of his life. At first he made numerous, unsentimental perspective drawings in charcoal of the local fishing community and painted portraits of his family and friends. In 1881 and 1882 he showed with various Brussels groups and at the Brussels and Paris Salons. With

Self-portrait with a Flowered Hat, 1883
Ostend, Mus.

JAMES ENSOR

L'Intrigue, 1890
Antwerp, Mus. Royal des B-A.

45

People in Masks Fighting
over a Hanged Man (detail) 1891
Antwerp, Mus. Royal des B-A.

Woman Eating Oysters, 1882, his palette became brighter and more luminous. But this picture was refused by the Brussels groups and also by the Antwerp Salon. This was the first of many rejections that eventually made Ensor a bitter opponent of officialdom.

Ensor's art became the expression of a home life made unhappy by ill-feeling between his parents, and of his grudge against society in general. In the next few years he produced several canvases, such as *The Drunkards*, 1883, that depicted social outcasts. In 1884 he was a founder member of an *avant-garde* Brussels art society, Les XX, formed to oppose the established groups L'Essor and La Chrysalide. During its nine years of existence, 1884-93, Les XX played an important role in helping new painters, both French and Belgian, to be seen and recognized.

At Les XX's first exhibition Ensor showed his *Scandalized Masks*, 1883. This was the first of his compositions in which masks, used for purposes of symbolism and satirical distortion, were the dominant motif. Ensor's fascination with masks and the macabre, reflected in his illustrations to the stories of Edgar Allan Poe, were manifestations of the general taste for the strange and the exotic that was prevalent in the late 19th century. In the 20th century his mask theme and its emotional overtones were taken up by Emil Nolde and the other artists of the German Expressionist movement Die Brücke.

In 1886 Ensor made his first etchings, and began a series of Rembrandtesque drawings of the life of Christ that pointed a parallel between the rejection of Christ and the rejection of his own art. This was most forcibly expressed in *The Entry of Christ into Brussels in 1889*, painted in 1888. A huge canvas of about $8\frac{1}{2}$ by 14 feet, the brush strokes strong, the color apparently arbitrary, it was refused by Les XX in 1889 and never placed on exhibition until the Ensor show in Brussels of 1929.

When Ensor could not count on showing even with Les XX, he was so discouraged that in 1893 he offered, without success, to sell for 8,500 francs the entire contents of his studio. He exhibited only occasionally with the group, La Libre Esthétique, that replaced Les XX in 1893. Skeletons, like the masks, became an obsessive theme, of which one of the most striking examples is *Skeletons Trying to Warm Themselves*, 1889. Ensor also painted a series of still-lifes of great vitality and rich coloring. He admired Watteau, Manet, and Turner, and in turn influenced not only the German Expressionists, but also Paul Klee, Marc Chagall, and the Surrealists.

Slowly Ensor began to be recognized. He held his first one-man show in Brussels in 1896, and three years later a retrospective exhibition in Paris. In the early years of the 20th century there were various Ensor shows in Antwerp, Brussels, Paris, and New York. In 1903 Ensor was made a knight of the Order of Leopold. By about 1900, however, his best work was behind him. He spent the half century remaining to him reworking previous themes. He was created a baron in 1929, but the honor was based on his earlier achievement. He stayed in Ostend through both World Wars, and died there on November 19, 1949, at the age of 89.

L. Tannenbaum Ensor New York and London, 1951
P. Haesaerts Ensor New York and London, 1957

PAUL GAUGUIN   1848-1903

A leader of the Symbolists in the reaction against naturalistic painting

Paul Gauguin was born in Paris in 1848 into a middle-class home. Three years later, after Louis Napoleon's *coup d'état*, the family sailed to South America. Gauguin's father died en route. He himself lived in Lima, Peru, until he was taken back to France at the age of seven. He went to school in Orléans and Paris, enlisted at 17 as a naval cadet, and stayed at sea until 1871. His mother having died four years earlier, he took a stockbroking job provided by his guardian. In the course of it he met Émile Schuffenecker, his continual support in later life.

Gauguin soon began to be interested in art, to draw, paint, and build up a collection of Impressionist pictures. Impressionism fascinated him. In 1876 he met and was impressed by Camille Pissarro. A painting of his own was accepted at the Paris Salon the same year, and from 1880 to 1886 he showed at the Impressionist group exhibitions.

In 1883 France suffered a financial crisis. Gauguin threw up his job to paint full time with Pissarro at Osny, near Pontoise. The next year he moved to Copenhagen with his Danish wife and his children, and put on an exhibition of his work which aroused very little interest in Denmark. Gauguin found himself without money, and his wife was forced to give French lessons to support herself and the children. After another exhibition had failed to materialize, he returned to Paris with his son Clovis and took work as a bill poster. Father and son were both ill. Eventually, placing Clovis in a boarding-house and selling part of his art collection to raise funds, Gauguin left for Brittany. There, in 1886, he stayed for the first of several times in the Pension Gloanec at Pont-Aven, painting with a fierce energy and determination. He met and quarreled with Edgar Degas, but made friends with the painter Charles Laval, and with a very young painter and theorist, Émile

The Seine at Pont d'Iéna, 1875
Paris, Mus. de l'Impressionnisme

Haymaking in Brittany, 1888
Paris, Mus. de l'Impressionnisme

The Yellow Christ, 1889
Buffalo, N. Y.,
Albright-Knox Art Gall.

Bernard. The mark of Impressionism on his style had already decreased. At the same time he was influenced by Paul Cézanne's recent paintings and by Japanese prints.

Haunted by a longing—possibly the legacy of his memories of Peru—to paint in some tropical country, Gauguin made an eight-month trip to the Panama Canal and Martinique with Charles Laval. Back in Paris in December, 1887, ill with fever and dysentery, he worked at pottery and various other forms of applied art in addition to his painting. An exhibition of his new paintings was unsuccessful, however, and within two months he returned to Brittany.

Out of his second Brittany period, there emerged a style and a system of ideas that were in direct antithesis to the painting from nature inherent in Impressionism, and of great significance in the development of European art. Talks with Émile Bernard provided Gauguin with some ready-made formulas for crystallizing his tentative solutions and vague searches. His own mental agility and acute perception carried him further. In *Still-life with Three Puppies*, 1888, the flat, unrepresentational, decorative element in his style began to reveal itself. *The Vision after the Sermon—Jacob Wrestling with the Angel*, which followed, consists of strong, flat colors organized into well-defined areas. In neither painting is there the least suggestion of a shadow.

Gauguin passed on his new style, eventually called Synthetism, or Pictorial Symbolism, to the young painters who were later known as the Nabis. He gave one of them, Paul Sérusier, a short painting lesson.

Meanwhile Gauguin exchanged paintings and frequent letters with Vincent van Gogh, whom he had first met in Paris in 1886. With great difficulty van Gogh now persuaded him to leave Brittany and go south to live with him in Arles. The experiment was not a success. The dissimilarity of their views on painting distressed them; Gauguin insisted that van Gogh should work from memory, which he found very difficult. After only two months matters reached a climax. One day van Gogh, over-excited, threatened his friend. Gauguin in alarm spent the night in a hotel and afterwards went away to Paris, leaving van Gogh in a state of mental and physical collapse.

He then spent three months in Paris, where he did painting, pottery, sculpture, and, with Bernard, a series of lithographs on Breton subjects, returning to Brittany in March, 1889. He stayed first at Pont-Aven with Laval and Sérusier, then at the more remote Le Pouldu with the Dutch amateur painter Meyer de Haan, who often generously settled bills for him. In the winters he would return to Paris, where he lived in the house of his old friend Schuffenecker and met and talked to the Symbolist poets and writers.

In 1889 he showed in Brussels with Les XX and was admired by the critic Octave Maus, if not by the scornful public. The same year, he and Schuffenecker organized an Impressionist and Symbolist group exhibition at the Café Volpini in Paris. Coinciding with the Paris World Exhibition, it impressed both the literary and artistic devotees of Symbolism.

At the World Exhibition itself Gauguin made frequent visits to the Javanese model village. His interest in the East and in Eastern art was reflected in his style.

Women of Tahiti (detail) 1891
Paris, Mus. de l'Impressionnisme

His plans to get to the tropics were ceaseless. Although he quarreled with Schuffe-necker and Bernard, he managed to arrange a successful auction of his paintings. The critic Octave Mirbeau was persuaded to write an introduction to the catalogue. So in April, 1891, feted by his friends, Gauguin set sail for Tahiti.

There he was soon on friendly terms with the natives and lived with a Tahitian girl, Tehura, some miles from Papeete. He was fascinated by the Tahitian way of life and its ancient culture. Glowing color pervaded his new canvases. But Gauguin's life in his "tropical paradise" was never easy. In February, 1892, he was very ill, and not much better by the end of the year. He worked until his painting materials gave out for lack of money, and had finally to apply for repatriation. Before he left Tahiti he painted *The Moon and the Earth*, a vivid expression of his feeling for the Maori culture, which he had read about in Moerenhout's book on Polynesian lore. The legends that he copied out from Moerenhout became the basis of his own book "Noa Noa," published in 1897.

The White Horse, 1898
Paris, Mus. de l'Impressionnisme

Back in Paris in 1893, Gauguin received an unexpected legacy from an uncle and was able to keep himself for a time in Paris and Brittany with a Javanese girl, Anna. But in a brawl over her with some sailors, his ankle was broken, his studio ransacked, and Anna abducted. So in 1895, after a second auction sale of his work, he went back to Tahiti and settled with another native girl, painting steadily despite his bad health.

During this last phase, his work gained a new breadth and something of a classical character. The vast *Where Do We Come From? What Are We? Where Are We Going?*, 1897, was the summary of his emotional response to life and his surroundings. At last his views on art clarified. He wrote to a friend: "Have always before you the Persians, the Cambodians, and a bit of the Egyptian. The great mistake is the Greek one, however beautiful it may be."

In 1898 Gauguin attempted, unsuccessfully, to commit suicide. Then he became a clerk in Papeete, came into conflict with the authorities, and published a satirical

Where Do We Come From? What Are We? Where Are We Going? 1897
Boston, Mass., Mus. of Fine Arts

broadsheet ridiculing the local Europeans. Even when he moved to the Marquesas Islands in 1901, he found no peace. Very ill, he continued to champion the natives against the European settlers. In March, 1903, he was fined and sentenced to three months imprisonment. He died on May 8, in loneliness and poverty.

Gauguin's impact on art was immeasurable. In the late 19th century he was a source for the Nabis, German Expressionism, and to some extent Art Nouveau, and he was one of the mainsprings of idealistic art the in 20th century.

J. Rewald Gauguin London, 1948
P. Gauguin The Intimate Journals London, 1952
C. Étienne Gauguin Geneva, 1953
R. J. Goldwater Gauguin London, 1957

Self-portrait, about 1888
Chicago, Art Inst.,
Joseph Winterbotham Coll.

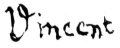

VINCENT VAN GOGH   1853-1890

A painter obsessed with the problems of expression

Vincent van Gogh was born in Zundert, in the Dutch province of Brabant, in 1853. He was the eldest son of a church minister, and felt from an early age that he should make preaching his life's work. But he also began drawing. On his first visit to London at the age of 20, and when he returned to England as a lay preacher three years later, he sent back drawings to his parents.

Meanwhile he visited Paris in 1874 and returned there the next year to work at the Goupil Gallery, of which his uncle was a director. After a short time he quarreled with the management and left. He then began his studies for the ministry, but failed to pass his examinations. Instead, late in 1878, he went to work as a lay preacher among the miners of the Borinage in Belgium. He was soon dismissed as unsuitable.

From this succession of disappointments van Gogh turned, at the age of 27, to art, staying on for a time in the Borinage. In October, 1880, he made his way to Brussels, where he took a short course at the Brussels Academy, and then went back to his parents in Etten, Holland. Some months later his disputes with them became insupportable and he went to The Hague. There he studied under a relative of his, the painter Anton Mauve. He spent the last three months of 1883 in the desolate countryside of Drenthe near the Dutch-German border, returning at the end of December to his parents, now in Nuenen.

Jean François Millet and Joseph Israels were the artists whom van Gogh most admired and copied. Like Millet he reproduced the life of the workers around him, executing an enormous number of studies of the miners of the Borinage, the poor of the almsh ouses and workhouse of The Hague and, the landscapes and peasants of Drenthe and Nuenen. Van Gogh's most important work of this period was *The Potato Eaters*, 1885, a Millet-type painting with a strong sacramental quality. Although his compositions were careful, it was the content of a picture that always took first place in his eyes. Interested in any artist with a social message to convey, he made a collection of English magazine illustrations. An emotional influence of a different sort in these years was his deep and unrequited attachment to his cousin Kee Vos-Stricker, a young widow with a small son.

Van Gogh began to be aware of the existence of Impressionism. He knew nothing about it, though he was interested in the color theories of Eugène Delacroix. He learned to appreciate Delacroix through his contact, on a short visit to Antwerp early in 1886, with the work of Rubens. During this visit, though living in extreme poverty, he discovered and began collecting Japanese prints. Touches of lighter pigment started to enliven the dark, heavy coloring of his earlier paintings. At the Antwerp Academy he learned nothing, since he refused to compromise with the professors over his forthright approach to drawing.

In February, 1886, he left Antwerp for Paris, where he stayed for two years, a period critical in his development. At last he was able to judge Impressionism for himself and to meet its exponents. He saw their work, and that of Camille Corot and Honoré Daumier, at the Goupil Gallery, where his brother Theo, an ardent and generous supporter of the Impressionists, worked. Henri de Toulouse-Lautrec did van Gogh's portrait. Camille Pissarro enthusiastically explained Pointillism to him. The art shop proprietor Père Tanguy let him have paints and canvas in exchange for his work. He also met Degas and Seurat and became friendly with Paul Signac, Gauguin and, in 1887, Émile Bernard.

Van Gogh spent hours in the Louvre and studied figure drawing with Fernand Cormon. But it was as he came to appreciate Impressionism that his color intensified and his handling grew freer. Living in Paris with Theo, his constant support to the end of his life, he painted flower studies, still-lifes, and landscapes. He gradually adopted from Signac and Seurat, though without their conscious science, a pointillist or neo-impressionist technique. In 1887 paintings by van Gogh were hung at the offices of "La Revue Indépendante," the restaurant La Fourche, and the lobby of the Théâtre Libre. He also organized an exhibition of his own work,

Sunflowers, 1888
London, N. G.

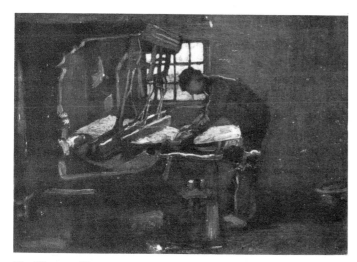
The Weaver, 1884
Otterlo, Holland, Kröller-Müller

The Artist's Bedroom at Arles, 1888
Chicago, Art Inst., Helen Birch Bartlett Memorial Coll.

Portrait of Armand Roulin, 1888
Rotterdam, Boymans-van Beuningen

and that of Bernard, Toulouse-Lautrec, and Louis Anquetin, at the cabaret Le Tambourin.

Life in Paris began to affect van Gogh's health. Suffering from depression, he took to heavy drinking. In any case he was too excitable for his brother to find it easy to live with him. In February, 1888, he left for Arles in Provence.

The south of France was as much a revelation to him as Paris had been. He worked in a frenzy, living alone as cheaply as possible and eating very little. Color and strong sunlight filtered into his painting, as he searched for a simpler, more powerful line and greater expression, through color, of moods and feelings. The necessity and the problems of a color symbolism preoccupied him. At this time he painted the *Night Café*, to him "a place where one can ruin oneself, go mad, or commit a crime."

Meanwhile Provence became for him the equivalent of Japan. He looked for Japanese motifs. A drawbridge, for example, or an orchard, recurs time and again in his work of this period. So do the "series," which he painted as parallels to the "series" that occur in Japanese prints. He made many drawings in pen and ink and experimented with textures of paint. In letters to Theo, Gauguin, and Bernard he spoke of plans for an artist's colony in the south of France. With Gauguin and Bernard he exchanged self-portraits in the Japanese custom. Portraiture began to assume great importance for him.

In September, 1888, having made up his mind that Gauguin should come south, van Gogh moved into the Yellow House in Arles. Gauguin left Brittany with reluctance and joined him there in October. He did not like Provence. Soon tensions arose between the two painters. Gauguin's method of working from memory irritated van Gogh. There were clashes and heated arguments. By December, when they visited Montpellier to see paintings by Delacroix and Gustave Courbet in the local museum, Gauguin was already thinking of returning to the north. This and the news that Theo was engaged to be married

The Drawbridge, 1888
Cologne, Wallraf-Richartz-Mus.

The Sower, 1888
Otterlo, Holland, Kröller-Müller

upset van Gogh. On December 24 he had his first mental seizure. Gauguin claimed afterwards that it was because van Gogh threatened him that he spent the night in a hotel. That evening van Gogh cut off part of his own left ear, to offer it to the prostitutes of the local brothel. He was taken to hospital, where he lay unconscious for three days.

From this time on, life became increasingly difficult for van Gogh. He suffered more or less frequent seizures, which eventually so perturbed him that, hoping to be cured and to avoid being a greater burden on the recently married Theo, he entered the Saint-Rémy asylum of his own free will. Periods of mental clarity alternated with attacks, so that he was able to produce many paintings and drawings both inside and outside the asylum grounds. He worked in a changed style, frenzied and turbulent, with cypress trees a persistent motif. To calm himself, he made many copies after Delacroix, Daumier, Rembrandt, and his consistent favorite, Millet. Although his tentative suggestion of joining Gauguin in Brittany was not encouraged, he was determined to return to the north of France.

In January, 1890, some of van Gogh's paintings were exhibited in Brussels with Les XX. An article on him appeared in "Mercure de France." In March, 1890, ten of his pictures were hung at the Salon des Indépendants in Paris, and highly praised. In May he was able to leave Saint-Rémy, pay a short visit to Paris to see Theo and his family, and settle at Auvers-sur-Oise under the watchful eye of Dr. Gachet, a friend of Pissarro and an amateur painter and collector. At first he painted with great determination in the surrounding countryside. Soon, worried about his brother's problems and his own chances of recovery, he reverted to his depression and quarreled with Dr. Gachet. His last turbulent paintings were of wheatfields. On July 27 he shot himself. Theo came down from Paris and on July 29, 1890, Vincent van Gogh died. Within a few years his paintings were as widely influential as any produced in his generation. The French Fauvists and the German Expressionists in particular were deeply indebted to him.

M. Schapiro Van Gogh New York, 1950: London, 1951
C. Nordenfalk Van Gogh London, 1953
D. Cooper Drawings and Watercolors by van Gogh London, 1955
V. van Gogh The Complete Collected Letters New York, 1958

Portrait of Dr. Gachet, 1890
Paris, Mus. de l'Impressionnisme

HIS WORKS INCLUDE

The Potato Eaters, 1885
*Amsterdam, Stedelijk Mus.,
V. W. van Gogh Coll.*

Père Tanguy, 1887
Paris, Mus. Rodin

Sunflowers, 1888
London, N. G.

Peach Trees in Blossom, 1889
London, Courtauld Inst. Gall.

Church at Auvers, 1890
Paris, Mus. de l'Impressionnisme

Crows over a Wheat Field, 1890
*Amsterdam, Stedelijk Mus.,
V. W. van Gogh Coll.*

See also pages 170, 171, 172, 173, 174, 175, 221, 222

CARL FREDRIK HILL   1849-1911

A Swedish landscape painter and imaginative draftsman

Carl Fredrik Hill was born in 1849 in Lund, southern Sweden. His father was a brilliant mathematician and a professor at Lund University. As a child Hill was studious and intelligent and showed a particular interest in landscape drawing. In 1871, after studying aesthetics for a year at Lund University, he entered the Stockholm Academy. During his two years there he acquired a great technical ability but also a dissatisfaction with academic theory.

On meeting fellow countrymen who had visited Paris, Hill learned of the latest

HIS WORKS INCLUDE

Landscape, 1877
Stockholm, Nationalmus.

Weird Rock Dwellings and Hovering Birds, after 1880
Stockholm, Nationalmus.

Standing Figure and Lyre, after 1880
Malmö, Sweden, Mus.

Temple Architecture with Tigers and Leopards, after 1880
Malmö, Sweden, Mus.

See also pages 185, 234

Temple Architecture with Tigers and
Leopards (detail) after 1880
Malmö, Sweden, Mus.

HILL

developments in French art. In 1873 he went to France to see for himself. The following summer, at the village of Barbizon, near Paris, he saw landscape paintings by Charles Daubigny, Narcisse Diaz de la Peña, Théodore Rousseau, Corot, and Courbet, in which he found the rich colors and the lively brushwork that he sought. He also admired the Impressionists, but his use of color, always closely linked with his emotions, was far more intense than theirs.

For some time his landscape style, though individual in feeling, was very like that of Corot. He had a painting accepted at the Paris Salon of 1875. However, by 1876 he had adopted a lighter, airy, "unfinished" style and his entry was refused at the Salon. By the next year his painting was calmer still, tending toward a classical composition based on strong verticals and horizontals. Dark foregrounds were contrasted with pale distances. Echoes of Corot were again apparent.

Hill's work had been noticed in 1876 by some of the Impressionists, who invited him to exhibit with them at their third group show in 1877. But that year he suffered his first mental crisis. In January, 1878, he was placed in an asylum in Paris, where he stayed until he was sent home to Lund in 1880.

He remained in Lund, cared for by his mother and sisters, until his death in 1911. His quiet, withdrawn existence there was broken only occasionally by a journey to Stockholm to see an exhibition or a play. The ink and crayon drawings that flowed steadily from his hand throughout these 30 years were based partly on life, partly on imagination. They possess a concentrated, visionary quality, lapsing from time to time into incoherence. Hill's varied subjects and styles over this period seem to have anticipated many modern movements and artists unknown to him, Henri Matisse and Pablo Picasso among them.

Self-portrait of the Artist
in a Rage, 1881
Bern, Kunstmus.

FERDINAND HODLER 1853-1918

A Swiss Symbolist and landscape painter

Ferdinand Hodler was born in Bern, Switzerland, in 1853, the son of a carpenter. When he was five his father died and his mother remarried. At the age of 14 he was apprenticed to a landscape artist in Thun, and when he was 18 he studied painting with another in Geneva. This was a training that was thorough rather than inspired, though it made him familiar with Hans Holbein the Younger, Rembrandt, and the landscapes of Camille Corot.

A journey to Spain in 1878 broadened Hodler's style, bringing him in touch with a mild form of Impressionism. His real interest, however, was in legend and history, his real feelings for the primitive and the tragic. These were reinforced in 1891 by a visit to Paris, where he came into contact with many new styles. He absorbed new ideas, especially those of Paul Gauguin and his followers and those of the Neo-Impressionist Georges Seurat. He became a Symbolist and his own "parallelist" principles consisted mainly in the rhythmic, repetitive use of line and shape in composition, with emphasis on their decorative and mystical elements. His paintings were in some ways comparable with those of the Symbolist Pierre

Puvis de Chavannes, who praised the *Procession of Wrestlers*, Hodler's prize-winning entry at the Paris World Exhibition in 1889. Hodler's color was brighter, however, and his forms more stylized than Puvis's.

In 1890 his *Night* caused a stir at the Paris Salon. He also met much violent criticism, particularly of his fresco designs for the Zurich Museum, which were finally accepted in 1899. In Germany there were many enthusiasts for his work, despite the fact that it gradually came dangerously near to sentimentality. He was awarded a gold medal at Munich in 1897 and admitted to the Berlin Sezession in 1899. At the Vienna Sezession of 1904 a large show was held in Hodler's honor. Within the next few years he received commissions from both the university of Jena and the city of Hanover. Apart from these large decorative commissions, his later works consisted chiefly of mountain landscapes, painted with arbitrary and expressive color. He died on May 20, 1918.

The Retreat after the Battle of Marignana, about 1900
Zurich, Kunsthaus

Lake Geneva from Chexbres, 1905
Basel, Öffentliche Kunstsamm.

WINSLOW HOMER   1836-1910

A realist painter and one of the first original American artists

Winslow Homer was born in 1836 in Boston. His ancestors were some of the earliest settlers in Massachusetts. At 19 he was apprenticed to John H. Bufford, the most distinguished lithographer in Boston, with whom he worked for two years. Thus he learned to draw by making illustrations for pictorial weekly magazines. For some years he worked for the Boston paper "Ballou's Pictorial." In 1859 he moved to New York. Refusing the post of staff artist offered him by "Harper's Weekly," he worked for the next 17 years as a freelance illustrator, though mostly for this magazine.

Homer could extract the utmost from the rather intractable medium of the woodcut, using firm outlines and broad masses of light and dark. His eye for a subject was always fresh. He would select anything that seemed to him to have pictorial value, whether he took it from fashionable society or from the New York streets. He accompanied the Union army in the Civil War, 1861-65, which he recorded in a series of drawings for "Harper's Weekly."

It was at this time that, almost entirely self-taught, he first experimented in oils, producing paintings low in tone and color, and with the same broad masses and clear line of his illustrations. One of them, *Prisoners from the Front*, was shown at the American National Academy of Design in 1866. It created a sensation and made Homer famous. At the Paris World Exhibition of 1867, one of his paintings that represented American art was admired by many critics.

During 1867 and 1868 Homer spent some months in France. He painted a little and visited the Louvre; one of his woodcuts shows students and enthusiasts making copies of the old masters. Certain paintings by Homer suggest that he learned something from Edgar Degas, but there is no doubt that he maintained and developed a style of his own, investigating the properties of light and color in a direction unexplored by the Impressionists, though in some ways parallel to Impressionism. Light did not dissolve his forms, but gave them monumentality and richness. This was so even when, in 1873, he took up watercolor and softened his forms. In this new medium he perfected an extraordinary breadth of handling.

In 1881 he made a sudden break and went to the north of England, where he lived in solitude for two years at Tynemouth on the coast. Back again in the United States, he settled at Prout's Neck, a desolate place on the Maine coast. A change in style accompanied the change in Homer's way of living. His earlier preference for children, young girls, and small everyday scenes as subjects was discarded in favor of the sea in all its aspects. He was concerned in particular with man's struggle against the elements, an obsession that gave his painting a new strength. Homer did not leave Maine again, except for yearly trips abroad that became an extension of

Canoe on the Rapids, 1897
Cambridge, Mass., Fogg Art Mus.

The Gulf Stream, 1899
New York, Met. Mus., Wolfe Fund

his exploration of nature. By the time he died, in 1910, he had worked out a personal vision of the interchange between man and nature, and a personal way of expressing it. He had also widened the scope of American painting and brought about a revolution in the use of watercolor.

L. Goodrich Winslow Homer New York, 1944

JOHAN BARTHOLD JONGKIND

1819-1891

A Dutch precursor of Impressionism

Johan Barthold Jongkind was an important figure in the development of Impressionism, particularly through his influence on Claude Monet. He was born at Lattrop, near Rotterdam, on June 3, 1819, and studied under the landscape painter Andreas Schelfhout at the Academy of The Hague. In 1845 he met Eugène Isabey, whose influence is to be seen in his early work. The following year he went to Paris, where he worked under Isabey and François Édouard Picot, exhibiting at the Paris Salon in 1848, and again in 1852. Two famous art critics and writers, first Charles Baudelaire and later Émile Zola, admired him and wrote of him in several magazines and newspapers.

Jongkind divided his time for some years between The Hague, Paris, and the Normandy coast. At an exhibition arranged by Count Doria, his works were exhibited with paintings by Corot, Daubigny, and Constant Troyon. He underwent great hardship, and also suffered from persecution mania and depressions. In 1860 Corot, Isabey, Théodore Rousseau, and François Bonvin organized a sale for his profit, and in the same year Monet commented on Jongkind's crazed state of mind in a letter to Eugène Boudin. When Jongkind was painting in Le Havre, he had been introduced to Monet, who in turn introduced him to Boudin in 1862. Jongkind was to play an important part in Monet's early development, exercising on him a more decisive influence than that of Boudin. He helped young Monet to develop his abilities, and to look closely and clearly at nature.

Jongkind's own style had matured by about 1860 and, although he did not do any outdoor painting in oils, he made vivid sketches and watercolors direct from nature, always trying to show exactly what he saw before him. In 1864 he painted two views of Notre Dame in Paris, one seen on a winter morning, the other at sunset. In this way the real subject of his paintings became the atmospheric conditions of the moment rather than the actual object before him.

In later years Jongkind traveled around France, Belgium, and Switzerland with his friend and pupil Mme. Fesser, who succeeded to some extent in calming his nervous state. They visited Lake Geneva and Isère, where Jongkind settled after 1880, though he paid occasional visits to Paris. His late works, including views of Isère, were very bold in color. Jongkind ended his life in a state of madness, dying at Côte-Saint-André, Isère, on February 9, 1891.

The Port, 1864
Brussels, Mus. Royaux des B-A.

HIS WORKS INCLUDE
Ruins of the Château de Rosemont
1861
Paris, Louvre
Beach at Sainte-Adresse, 1863
Paris, Mus. de l'Impressionnisme
La Ciotat, 1880
Rotterdam, Boymans-van Beuningen
View of Overschie
Rotterdam, Boymans-van Beuningen

See also page 212

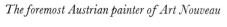

The foremost Austrian painter of Art Nouveau

The son of a Bohemian engraver, Gustav Klimt was born on July 14, 1862, in Baumgarten near Vienna. He attended the Vienna Academy between the ages of 14 and 22, then worked in collaboration with his brother Ernst and the painter Matsch on decorations for the Vienna Kunsthistorisches Museum and theaters in Vienna, Fiume (now Rijeka in Yugoslavia) and, in Czechoslovakia, Karlsbad and Reichenberg. The death of Ernst in 1892 brought the partnership to an end and left Klimt incapable of painting for almost six years.

When he took up his brush again in 1897, his style had completely altered. From 1890 onward he had had the opportunity to see Impressionist, Neo-Impressionist, Pointillist, and Symbolist pictures at exhibitions in Vienna. These, and his contact with works of the English Pre-Raphaelite Brotherhood, the American James McNeill Whistler, the Dutchman Jan Toorop, and German "Jugendstil," provided Klimt with the stimulus he needed to develop a specifically Austrian form of Art Nouveau. When the Vienna Sezession was founded in 1897 to promote this new style, Klimt was its first president. By contributing articles and drawings to the journal "Ver Sacrum" (Sacred Spring), which was founded for the same purpose, he also brought Art Nouveau to Austrian book illustration.

The problems that preoccupied him, however, were still those connected with interior decoration. The three ceiling decorations commissioned from him for the university of Vienna, 1900-3 (destroyed in 1945), showed how Art Nouveau could

Portrait of a Woman, about 1897
Oberlin, Ohio, Memorial Art Mus.

Malcesine on Lake Garda
Vienna, Österreichische Gal.

The Three Ages of Woman (detail)
Rome, Gall. Naz. d'Arte Moderna

be adapted to the demands of monumental painting. When the authorities refused to erect them, Klimt himself bought them back. In a frieze of the same period, intended as a free interpretation of Beethoven's Ninth Symphony and exhibited at the Sezession, the slender, expressive figures echo paintings by the Pre-Raphaelites and by Edvard Munch.

In 1905 Klimt left the Sezession. From 1905 to 1908 he collaborated on a mural in mosaic and enamel on marble for the dining room of the Stoclet Palace in Brussels. The various media employed in this mural included tempera and gold and silver leaf. Klimt was making extensive use of spiral forms at this time, and arranging his figures in such a way that the spaces between them became as important as the figures themselves. In 1908 he was awarded a gold medal in Rome, and started the Klimt Group. At about this time he began to intensify his colors and his designs, building up tension by presenting the contrast between flat and plastic forms.

Two years later a Klimt retrospective exhibition was held at the Venice Biennale. In 1917 Klimt was made an honorary member of the Vienna and Munich Academies. The following year, on February 6, he died in Vienna, having paved a way for modern Austrian art.

HIS WORKS INCLUDE

Portrait of Madame Riedler, 1906
Vienna, Österreichische Gal.

The Kiss, about 1909
Strasbourg, Mus. des B-A.

Adam and Eve, 1918
Vienna, Österreichische Gal.

See also pages 204, 239

WILHELM LEIBL   1844-1900

A German portraitist and genre painter

Wilhelm Leibl was born on October 23, 1844, in Cologne, where his father was director of music at Cologne Cathedral. In 1861 he began to study under a local painter and three years later went to Munich Academy. Between 1866 and 1869 he made further studies under two different painters. He then exhibited for the first time in Munich. His early work was heavily influenced by Dutch painting. He chose everyday subjects, which he treated entirely without the sentiment and romanticism typical of contemporary German art.

In 1869 Leibl lived for nine months in Paris, working with Gustave Courbet and thus strengthening his attachment to realism. The Franco-Prussian war made it necessary for him return to Germany. In 1870 he was awarded the Paris gold medal for his *Portrait of Frau Gedon*, in which Rembrandt's influence is clearly discernible.

He stayed in Munich from 1870 to 1873, then at various small villages in Bavaria, living in the same way as his peasant neighbors and painting the scenes around him. He still viewed his subjects with great matter-of-factness; no detail escaped his careful, perfect draftsmanship. This element of his mature work was to influence the New Objectivists of the 1920's, their figure studies and portrait drawing in particular.

From 1878 to 1881 Leibl made his home in the little Bavarian town of Berbling, where he painted *Three Women in Church*. He moved to Aibling and then, in 1892,

Unevenly Matched, about 1877
Frankfurt-am-Main,
Städelsches Kunstinst.

HIS WORKS INCLUDE

The Critics, 1868
Vienna, Österreichische Gal.

Cocotte, 1869
West Berlin, Staatl. Mus.

Three Women in Church, 1881
Hamburg, Kunsthalle

See also page 194

59

W. Leibl.

to Kutterling. He died in Würzburg on December 4, 1900. Although his subjects remained free to the end from any trace of romantic idealism, Dutch art failed to retain its hold on him in his later years. He then achieved a kind of personal impressionism characterized by a stronger, broader, though always delicate, technique.

Self-portrait, 1925
West Berlin, Staatl. Mus.

MAX LIEBERMANN   1847-1935

A realist painter who brought Germany into contact with contemporary French and Dutch art

Max Liebermann was born in Berlin on July 20, 1847, the son of a German-Jewish businessman. He studied under a local painter and in 1869 enrolled at the Weimar School of Art. Three years later, at the age of 25, he exhibited for the first time, showing a painting, *Woman Plucking Geese*, that was dark in color and simple in construction. After a few months in Paris he spent the following summer in Barbizon, meeting Millet and seeing works by Corot, Courbet, Troyon, and Daubigny. The result was a perceptible brightening of his palette. The impression made on him by the realism of Millet and Courbet was a lasting one. His position in German painting was the equivalent of Millet's in the development of French art.

Liebermann next went to Holland, where he made a careful study of Frans Hals and allowed the influence of Joseph Israels to strengthen his realist convictions. The visit seems to have opened his eyes for the first time to the possibilities of light and atmosphere. At this period his subjects, very similar to Millet's, were drawn mainly from orphanages and old people's homes. When he moved to Munich in 1878 his realistic painting *Christ in the Temple* aroused much criticism and was

Brother and Sister, 1876
Dresden, Gemäldegal.

The Netmenders, 1889
Hamburg, Kunsthalle

condemned by the clergy as irreverent. He did not try a religious subject again. In 1884 he settled once more in Berlin, returning to Holland for some months of every year until World War I.

The Impressionist movement had no visible effect on Liebermann's style until after 1890, when he was much attracted by the work of Édouard Manet. His palette became considerably more luminous and his handling of paint more fluid. But he was never an Impressionist in the strict sense of the word, for he never allowed light or color to dominate a picture. Instead, with Lovis Corinth, he became a leader of the Berlin Sezession of 1899 and helped to make it an effective channel of French influence into Germany. Through him, German painters turned away from their bourgeois sentimentality to a realism linked with the French tradition, and German art was back in the stream of modern developments.

Liebermann's first personal success was a medal awarded at the 1881 Paris Salon for *An Asylum for Old Men*. Later he became president of the Berlin Academy. In 1897 and 1907 exhibitions of his work were held in honor of his 50th and 60th birthdays. In 1910 he came briefly into contact with Oskar Kokoschka. But although Liebermann to some extent influenced the Expressionist Max Beckmann, he could not understand the new art that was in process of evolution. He even helped to exclude Emil Nolde's work from the exhibition of the Berlin Sezession in that year. He died in Berlin in 1935.

HIS WORKS INCLUDE

The Pig Market
Mannheim, Städtische Kunsthalle

The Netmenders, 1889
Hamburg, Kunsthalle

Oude Vinck
Zurich, Kunsthaus

Country Bar in Bavaria
Paris, Mus. d'Art Moderne

At the Uhlenhorster Ferryhouse, 1910
Hamburg, Kunsthalle

See also page 195

ARISTIDE MAILLOL   1861-1944

A French sculptor of imposing female nudes

Aristide Maillol was born on December 8, 1861, at Banyuls in the Pyrenees, where his family lived by fishing and growing vines. This Mediterranean environment may account for his later admiration for ancient sculpture. He went to school in Banyuls and to college in Perpignan, where he copied plaster casts at the city museum. At 21 he went to Paris. His teacher at the École des Beaux-Arts, the painter Jean Léon Gérôme, sent him on to the École des Arts Décoratifs, where he was a pupil of Alexandre Cabanel for four years.

The objects of Maillol's most careful study were the pictures in the Louvre and the medieval tapestries in the Cluny museum. The paintings of his contemporaries Pierre Puvis de Chavannes and Paul Gauguin gave direction to his own painting and pointed out to him the need for the decorative elements to predominate in a work of art. He decided to manufacture tapestries and to that end started a small studio in Banyuls, employing village girls on the weaving and using home-made dyes. Gauguin admired a tapestry of his shown in Brussels in 1894 with Les XX and later in Paris.

Maillol moved to Paris in 1895 and settled three years afterwards in Villeneuve-Saint-Georges. He had great difficulty in making a living, until friends recommended him to a wealthy patron, who commissioned several tapestries. During

Action Unchained: from the Monument to Blanqui, about 1906
London, Tate

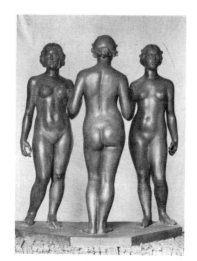

The Three Nymphs, about 1938
London, Tate, et al.

HIS WORKS INCLUDE

Dancers, 1898
Paris, Mus. d'Art Moderne

Pomona, 1937
Paris, Petit-Palais

The Three Nymphs, about 1938
London, Tate, et al.

See also page 252

their fabrication Maillol's eyesight weakened and for several months he was completely blind. In order to save the strain on his eyes, he turned instead to sculpture, producing carvings and terracottas that at first reflected, then reacted against, the style of Auguste Rodin.

In about 1900 the painter Édouard Vuillard brought his friend Ambroise Vollard to Villeneuve-Saint-Georges. The young dealer bought some sculptures, which he then had cast in bronze, and in 1902 organized a Maillol exhibition in Paris, at which Rodin acquired a bronze figurine and the *Leda* was sold to the critic Octave Mirbeau. Maillol began to show regularly at the Paris Salon d'Automne and attracted attention which sometimes took the form of virulent criticism. His entry for a competition in 1903 for a monument to the writer Émile Zola was rejected in favor of Constantin Meunier's.

In 1908, with his German friend and patron Count Kessler, Maillol traveled to Greece by way of Naples and Pompeii. This journey reinforced his feeling for early Greek art, very evident in the version of *Pomona* that he submitted to the Salon d'Automne of 1910. He then received the commission for a monument to Cézanne.

His work was interrupted by World War I when, through his association with Count Kessler, he was accused, though not convicted, of spying. His large postwar commemorative statues included a monument to the dead of Banyuls. He also spent some time in later life producing woodcut and lithograph illustrations to Latin authors. He died in October, 1944, after a road accident near Banyuls.

Maillol's sculpture was closely related to the female human form, which he represented in simple, solid, basic volumes, never allowing his instinct for decorative line to predominate. Renoir, who took to sculpture late in life, was influenced by him, just as he had been influenced by Renoir's paintings.

J. Rewald Maillol New York and London, 1939

ÉDOUARD MANET

1832-1883

A revolutionary despite himself

Édouard Manet was born in Paris on January 25, 1832, the son of a wealthy lawyer. On leaving school at the age of 16 he joined the navy. He would have preferred to study painting, however, and in 1850 his father at last allowed him to enroll as a pupil of the history painter Thomas Couture, with whom he remained for six years.

Manet's revolutionary *Absinthe Drinker*, submitted to the Paris Salon of 1859, was rejected by the jury, though the great Romantic painter Eugène Delacroix protested on his behalf against their decision. In 1861, influenced by Spanish pictures and fascinated by Spanish subject-matter, Manet offered *The Guitarist* to the Salon. It was accepted, and praised by the poet and art critic Théophile Gautier. Another poet-critic, Charles Baudelaire, was a friend of the young painter, and wrote an article on him in 1862.

At the Salon des Refusés of April, 1863, Manet showed *Le Déjeuner sur l'Herbe*, for

EDGAR DEGAS
Portrait of Édouard Manet, about 1864
New York, Met. Mus., Rogers Fund

which nude and clothed figures had posed in the studio. The reaction of the public to this was a mixture of hilarity and indignation. Only one month before, however, an exhibition of Manet's paintings had made a profound impression on Claude Monet, who, with others of the younger, more adventurous artists, began to think of him as a leader. The writer Émile Zola—a champion of these young *avant-garde* painters—published a series of articles on Manet in 1865, prophesying a place for him in the Louvre.

Manet had been acquainted with Edgar Degas, with whom he had much in common, since 1862. But he did not really get to know Zola, Cézanne, Monet, or Pissarro until 1866, when he began to join in the discussions at the Café Guerbois in Paris. Later, from about 1876, a table was kept reserved for him and Degas and their friends at the Café de la Nouvelle-Athènes.

It was partly through Manet's inspiration that the Impressionist movement came about. But despite entreaties from Monet and pressure from Degas, he would not exhibit with the Impressionists at any of the group shows held by them between 1874 and 1886. To Degas's scorn and annoyance he desired only official recognition, feeling—a conviction that he never lost—that the Salon was the proper place for a painter to make his name. To it he submitted his work, often refused, right up to the year before his death. His fear of offending the authorities was such that when, in 1876, he was approached by a group of students from the Paris École des Beaux-Arts who wished to work under his direction, he declined to take them on.

Nor did he ever adopt the Impressionist manner without reserve. He never abandoned the love of black on which the stark effectiveness of *The Absinthe Drinker*,

The Fifer, 1866
Paris, Mus. de l'Impressionnisme

Concert in the Tuileries, 1862
London, N. G.

his first important picture, had depended. His colorful illusions about Spain were destroyed by a two-week visit to the country in August, 1865. This left him determined to record contemporary Paris with as immediate a realism as that with which Spanish painters like Velázquez and Francisco de Goya had presented the life of their own people. He painted scarcely one more Spanish scene. Instead he put something of Goya's grim *Executions of May 3, 1808* into *The Execution of Emperor Maximilian*. He made several versions of this picture soon after the news of the emperor's death in 1867. It was officially barred from the Paris World Exhibition of 1867, at which Manet, like Gustave Courbet, displayed his paintings in a pavilion of his own. In quite another vein, but again inspired by Goya, was Manet's *The Balcony*, 1868. After the Franco-Prussian war of 1870-71, in which he enlisted as a staff officer in the National Guard, he visited Holland and developed a deep admiration for the work of Frans Hals.

Manet's contact with the Impressionists was by no means entirely fruitless so far as his own style was concerned. He met Berthe Morisot, the first woman Impressionist, in 1868. She posed that year for *The Balcony*, and in 1874 she married his younger brother, Eugène. Through her example Manet's style, from the year he met her, became more highly colored and fluid. In the summer of 1868 he painted some seascapes at Boulogne with a new, free manner. He was also influenced by Japanese prints, lately discovered by the Paris *avant garde* and at one time or another the model of most of the Impressionists. A print by Utagawa Kuniaki can be seen in the background of his *Portrait of Émile Zola*, shown at the Salon of 1868.

Manet later spent some time painting at Argenteuil on the river Seine outside

The Execution of Emperor Maximilian, 1867
Mannheim, Städtische, Kunsthalle

The Croquet Match, 1873
Frankfurt-am-Main, Städelsches Kunstinst.

Paris with Monet, whom he helped out of dire financial circumstances with a loan of 1000 francs in 1878. It was Monet who encouraged him to paint out-of-doors rather than in the studio. Manet's palette brightened steadily from about 1873. In the summer of 1881, two years before he died, he was painting Versailles with the thoroughgoing naturalism of the Impressionists.

With the success of his Dutch-inspired *Le Bon Bock* at the Salon of 1873, his work had become less difficult to sell. However, when the singer Émilie Ambre took *The Execution of Emperor Maximilian* with her on a concert tour of the United States late in 1879, only the American press was enthusiastic. There was no response from the public, and the canvas had to be taken back to France. In April of the next year Manet held a one-man show in Paris at the offices of the review "La Vie Moderne." At the 1881 Salon he was awarded a second class medal.

All in all Manet was a disappointed man, and his health was failing. Nomination to the Legion of Honor in 1882, too late to be of any real encouragement, only aggravated his bitterness.

Yet despite this, he painted at the end of his life the picture that many consider to be his masterpiece, *The Bar at the Folies Bergères*, 1882. In the spring of 1883 his left leg was amputated. Gangrene set in, and he died in Paris on April 30, 1883. The next year a large memorial exhibition was held at the École des Beaux-Arts, and his reputation began to rise.

G. H. Hamilton   *Manet and his Critics*   *New Haven, Conn., 1954*
J. Richardson   *Manet*   *London, 1958*

The Waitress (La Servante de Bocks)
1879
London, N. G.

HANS VON MARÉES   1837-1887

The most original German painter of the 19th century

Hans von Marées was born in Elberfeld, Germany, on December 24, 1837. Demonstrating an early talent for painting, he was sent at the age of 16 to the Berlin Academy. He left with a thorough training as a draftsman but small experience of painting. In 1857, then aged 20, he settled in Munich and worked on his own.

His subjects were largely country scenes, painted in a realistic manner overlaid with sentimentality. More important at this time were his portraits, notably the *Portrait of the Artist's Father*, 1862, and the *Self-portrait with Lenbach*, 1863. *The Bath of Diana*, also of 1863, was unusual in Germany for its richness and warmth of color.

In 1864 Marées was helped out of a financial crisis by a Baron Schack of Munich, who bought one of his pictures and sent him to Italy to copy old masters. In Rome, where he lived from 1865, the impact of Renaissance art overwhelmed him. He made copies of Titian, Raphael, and Velázquez, feeling that he must learn to paint again from the beginning and that his progress hitherto had been worthless.

He broke with Baron Schack, but was rescued once more from financial diffi-

Self-portrait in a Kimono, 1872
Dresden, Gemäldegal.

The Bethrothal, about 1882
West Berlin, Staatl. Mus.

HIS WORKS INCLUDE

Portrait of the Artist's Father, 1862
Munich, Neue Pin.

St. Martin, 1869
West Berlin, Staatl. Mus.

Roman Vigna, 1871
Hamburg, Kunsthalle

The Garden of the Hesperides, 1885
Munich, Neue Pin.

See also page 198

culties by the generosity of a friend, Konrad Fiedler, who supported him from 1868. In 1869 they traveled together to Spain, France, and Holland, a journey that provided the second turning point in Marées's career and brought to his work a more direct realism of subject, color, and composition. Side by side with this remained his own inherent idealism, his Romantic emotion.

After service in the Franco-Prussian war of 1870 to 1871, Marées lived for a time in Berlin and Dresden. Now, in addition to numerous, often striking commissioned portraits and several self-portraits, he painted evocative idylls from his memories of the Roman countryside. When he returned to Italy in 1873 to decorate the library walls of the recently built Naples Zoological Institute, he took for the subject of his large frescoes the Neapolitan life around him. Out of its everyday simplicity he wrought the most powerful series of frescoes to be produced in the 19th century. They were finished in four months.

In 1874 Marées settled in Florence with a sculptor who had been his colleague at the Zoological Institute. He also made friends with the Swiss Romantic painter Arnold Böcklin, who had moved to Florence the same year. Marées died in Rome on June 5, 1887, at the age of 49.

His last works; rich in light and color, reverted again and again to the idyllic theme of nudes in a landscape. This depiction of a symbolic, instinctive interaction of man and nature provided a foretaste of the Expressionism of the 20th century.

The Sisters (watercolor and gouache)
Glasgow, Art Gall., Burrell Coll.

JAKOB MARIS   1837-1899

A member of the Hague school

Jakob Maris was born in The Hague in 1837, the son of a poor printer. His two younger brothers, Matthijs and Willem, also became painters but Jakob is generally considered to be the strongest artist of the three. At 21 he was apprenticed to the painter Johann Anthonis Stroebel and he later attended the Academies at The Hague and Antwerp. From 1865 to 1871 he lived in Paris.

Throughout the 1860's Maris's paintings were almost entirely sentimental in character, as demonstrated in *The Shepherdess*, 1868. However, the work he saw in Paris of the Barbizon School (then at the height of its activity) made a deep and lasting impression on him. In 1870 he painted *The Ferryboat*, thus indicating his change of interest from figure to landscape painting. After his return to The Hague in 1871 he quickly developed a style of landscapes and town views for which he became widely known. The view of *Dordrecht* is a typical work, with its large expanse of cloudy sky above the low, horizontal band of houses and water. While in his earlier works color tended to be dark and of little importance, following his stay in Paris he gradually changed to a palette of lighter and clearer tones with which he often achieved remarkable quality. In addition to his town and coastal views Maris painted mildly social realist subjects, such as *Plow and Horses*, 1880, showing the Dutch peasantry at work on the land.

Over the years Maris attained a leading position in the Hague school. This group of artists was much admired by the young Vincent van Gogh; he met and helped Maris while working in the Paris branch of Goupil's gallery, and Maris' name is mentioned several times in letters to Rappard during the 1880's. Later too, when he came to paint *The Drawbridge*, van Gogh evidently remembered and was influenced by Maris's painting of the same subject.

HIS WORKS INCLUDE

A Bleaching Yard, 1870
Amsterdam, Rijksmus.
View of Montigny - sur - Loing, 1870
Rotterdam, Boymans-van Beuningen
The Wooden Bridge, 1878
Amsterdam, Rijksmus.
Plow and Horses, 1880
New York, coll. Max Pam

See also page 184

CONSTANTIN MEUNIER   1831-1905

An artist concerned with a new social realism

Constantin Meunier was born on April 12, 1831, in Etterbeek, a suburb of Brussels. He first came into contact with artists in his mother's boarding house, and later he attended the Brussels Academy, where he studied sculpture under Charles Auguste Fraikin. He was, however, also attracted to painting and went to the atelier run by François Joseph Navez. At this stage Meunier's style was insipid and academic.

Meunier first exhibited at the Brussels Salon in 1851. About three years later he abandoned sculpture and turned to painting, possibly on the advice of Charles de Groux, with whom he became friendly. Together they frequented the Saint-Luc Studio, and Meunier was certainly influenced by his friend. He made designs for stained glass and fabrics, and produced many religious paintings. These clearly

The Miner: from the Monument to Labor
Brussels, Mus. Royaux des B-A.

A Fisherman on a Horse
Brussels, Mus. Royaux des B-A.

The Crab Catcher
Stockholm, Nationalmus.

67

See also page 247

reveal the influence of Millet and Courbet. Meunier frequently stayed in the Westmalle Trappist monastery, where he made studies for many pictures, including *The Burial of a Trappist Monk*, 1860.

In 1862 Meunier married, and settled down to a happy domestic life. He turned to historical painting and produced a series, *Episodes of the Peasants' War*. The turning point of his career was the discovery, in 1878, of the industrial world and its pictorial possibilities. Four years later his work was interrupted by a government mission to Spain, but he returned in 1883 to Brussels. He was appointed professor at the Louvain Academy of Fine Arts. In 1885 he again took up sculpture, in which he carried on the industrial subject-matter of his later paintings. His vast *Monument to Labor*, which was acquired by the Belgian government, remained unfinished. In 1893 he collaborated with the sculptor Karel van der Stappen on a scheme of decorations for the Brussels Botanical Gardens and with the Frenchman Félix Maurice Charpentier on a monument to Émile Zola. Meunier exhibited in Paris on several occasions. His social realism, part of a widespread movement on the continent of Europe in reaction to academic 19th-century art, has been particularly influential in East European countries. His approach offers a parallel to the early works of Vincent van Gogh. His technique was an innovation in the history of Belgian sculpture. He represented scenes of the life of the miners, and the misery of the working people from the industrial areas of Belgium.

Self-portrait
Cherbourg, Mus. des B-A.

JEAN FRANÇOIS MILLET   1814-1875

A painter and draftsman of outstanding directness and simplicity

Jean François Millet, the second of eight children, spent his youth in a village near Gréville in Normandy. His father was a farm laborer and led the music in the parish church, so that a sense of the interaction of religion and life was instilled into the young Jean François. He never lost his devoutness, nor his desire to interpret the Bible in terms of the life of the French laborer, much as Rembrandt had done with the life of the Dutch townspeople around him.

Millet worked for some time in the fields with his father. But his talent for drawing revealed itself, and at the age of 18 he began his studies under a minor painter in Cherbourg. Five years later he went to Paris, to the studio of a Romantic painter, Paul Delaroche. But he learned far more from the works of the Venetians and Michelangelo and Nicolas Poussin. He did not enjoy Paris. Apparently he kept to himself, avoiding his fellow students, who included Thomas Couture, the future teacher of Édouard Manet. Millet was always short of money, and in order to maintain himself produced small, sensuous oils or pastels in the style of Fragonard, Boucher, or Antoine Watteau, which he could sell to dealers for a few francs.

Millet returned to Cherbourg and Le Havre for a period, and then lived in Paris until it was struck by cholera in 1849. He moved to Barbizon on the edge of the Forest of Fontainebleau. There he stayed for the rest of his life, leading a quiet existence with his wife and children. At Barbizon he met the painters Théodore Rousseau and, at Rousseau's house, Diaz de la Peña. These three, with Charles Daubigny, united in their aim to concentrate on painting peasant life and country scenery, became known as the Barbizon School. Other visitors to Rousseau's house were the sculptor Antoine Louis Barye and the satirical painter and lithographer Honoré Daumier.

In 1850 Millet submitted *The Sower* and *The Binders* to the Salon, where they caused a small stir. The solidity and simplicity of *The Sower* were indeed remarkable, and in the contemporary context of academic art particularly striking. Although this painting was drawn mainly from memories of Normandy, its transcription of nature was accurate, direct, and powerful. In fact, the usual Barbizon practice of making studies on the spot helped to create and inspire the realism that culminated in Impressionism. Millet himself influenced many artists, most notably Vincent van Gogh, a passionate admirer and imitator, Georges Seurat, and Camille Pissarro.

From this time Millet was able to exhibit at the Salon. In 1885 *The Grafter* won the praise and enthusiasm of the writer Théophile Gautier. Many outstanding paintings followed, including *The Angelus*, 1859, and *The Man with a Hoe*, 1863. There were also numerous strong, sensitive charcoal drawings and a few experimental etchings. In 1860 Millet found a dealer to take his work in exchange for an agreed monthly sum, so that he was no longer in total poverty. Only his bad health prevented him from carrying out a state commission for eight paintings to decorate the Panthéon in Paris. He died in Barbizon in January, 1875.

Going to Work, about 1850
Glasgow, Art Gall.

HIS WORKS INCLUDE

The Binders, 1850
Paris, Louvre

The Gleaners, 1857
Paris, Louvre

The Buckwheat Harvest
Boston, Mass., Mus. of Fine Arts

The Angelus, 1859
Paris, Louvre

See also page 211

The Church at Gréville
Paris, Louvre

The Angelus, 1859
Paris, Louvre

CLAUDE MONET (photo)

Claude Monet

CLAUDE MONET

One of the most important of the Impressionist painters

Claude Monet was born in Paris on February 14, 1840, the son of a grocer, who took his family five years later to Le Havre, on the Seine estuary. The young Monet soon revealed a talent for drawing and made a name for himself in Le Havre by doing caricatures. The shop window where they were often displayed also contained sea paintings by Eugène Boudin, which Monet disliked intensely. But when by chance he met Boudin himself, he was persuaded, though reluctantly, to go sketching with him. Monet's attitude toward art was transformed by this confrontation with the possibility of painting in the open air, direct from the subject. He also began a collection of Japanese prints, which he maintained until the end of his life.

In 1859, at the age of 19, Monet went to Paris. That year he visited the Salon several times. He refused to return home or to enter the École des Beaux-Arts, but began instead at the Atelier Suisse, where Gustave Courbet had worked and Camille Pissarro sometimes came. At a dealer's exhibition the following year, Monet noticed pictures by Courbet, Eugène Delacroix, and the work of the Barbizon School. Meanwhile he often found members of Courbet's circle airing their ideas at the Brasserie des Martyrs.

Monet's military service interrupted his life in Paris. Two years in Algeria in an African regiment made him seriously ill, and his father was forced to buy him out of the four years that remained. He returned home to Le Havre, where he met the Dutch painter Johan Barthold Jongkind, eventually an even stronger influence on him than Boudin.

Back in Paris at the end of 1862, Monet enrolled, at his parents' wish, in Charles Gleyre's studio at the École des Beaux-Arts. Even at this stage he was a conscious rebel against the established canons of painting. He and his fellow students, Bazille, Renoir, and Sisley, formed a group apart from the others. In 1863 they spent Easter together at Chailly in the Fontainebleau Forest, painting tree studies in the open air. Gleyre's studio shut down at the end of that year.

Route du Bas-Breau in the Forest of Fontainebleau
1865   *Paris, Louvre*

Green Park, London, 1871
Philadelphia, Pa., Mus. of Art, Coll. W. P. Wilstach

70

By the beginning of 1865 Monet was very short of money. Bazille let him share his Paris studio. Then Monet had two views of the Seine estuary hung at the 1865 Salon. His name was confused by some of the spectators with that of Édouard Manet, who was startled and irritated to be complimented on Monet's work. Monet for his part had been an admirer of Manet since the Salon des Refusés of 1863 and was planning a huge *Le Déjeuner sur l'Herbe* to rival his. Unlike Manet's, it was to be painted as far as possible in the open air. In the forest at Chailly he made preliminary studies and began the final composition. But Courbet, whose freedom of brushwork he had learned to follow, came to visit him and suggested alterations that he accordingly made and afterwards regretted. He abandoned the canvas and later painted a portrait of one of his sitters, his mistress Camille Doncieux, to take its place at the Salon of 1866. This was accepted, described by the writer Émile Zola as full of energy and life, and praised by many other reviewers.

This temporary success persuaded Monet's parents to renew his allowance. He was able to paint some views of Paris, experimenting with color and light, and his ambitious *Women in the Garden*, the first exact record of outdoor light falling upon figures. It was over eight feet high, and had to be lowered into a trench dug in the garden to enable him to paint the top.

In 1867 he was again in acute financial difficulties. Bazille bought *Women in the Garden*, arranging to pay for it in instalments over four years so that Monet should have an income. Even this did not save the situation. The picture was rejected at the 1867 Salon, and Camille was expecting a child. Monet was obliged to return home for the summer, leaving her in Paris, where she gave birth to Jean Monet. His circumstances were so hopeless that Monet was near to attempting suicide.

The following years were not much better. He often could not afford paints, and sometimes what he had been able to do was appropriated by his creditors. But in Paris at the Café Guerbois, a meeting place for painters and writers where technical questions were frequently discussed, he was inspired to make further experi-

La Gare Saint-Lazare, 1877
Paris, Mus. de l'Impressionnisme

Snow Effects at Vétheuil, about 1878
Paris, Mus. de l'Impressionnisme

71

Regatta at Argenteuil (detail) 1872
Paris, Mus. de l'Impressionnisme

ments. With Sisley and Pissarro he concentrated on winter landscapes. And in Bougival on the Seine he and Renoir made a study of the effect of light on water. When Renoir too was desperate, Monet encouraged him.

In June, 1870, just before the outbreak of the Franco-Prussian war, Monet married Camille. In the autumn he fled to London. There he was introduced to Durand-Ruel, a dealer who was to be for many years the chief patron of Impressionism. Pissarro was also in London, and he and Monet painted together in the open air and saw the Constables and Turners in the museums. After the war, and a visit to Holland, Monet returned to France to settle with Camille in Argenteuil, on the Seine near Paris. A studio boat was built so that he could watch the light on the water. Renoir sometimes worked with him, and in the summer of 1874 they were joined by Manet, who was finally persuaded to overcome his prejudice against painting out-of-doors.

Monet was largely responsible for the first group show of the Impressionists, held in Paris in 1874. It was his painting *Impression: Sunrise*, 1872, that gave a focal point to the ridicule roused by the exhibition and its name to the Impressionist movement. For the next few years he was still in financial straits. With some help from Manet he struggled on. His second son, Michel, was born in 1878; in the autumn of 1879 Camille died.

In desperation, Monet submitted work to the Salon in 1880, for the first time for ten years. One painting was accepted. That year he also had a show of his own, and things became a little easier. Accused by Edgar Degas of pandering to officialdom, he did not exhibit at the Salon again. But he exhibited in most of the Impressionist group shows, several times in London, in Brussels with Les XX, and in New York when Durand-Ruel took 50 of his canvases there. To the dealer's annoyance, he also showed in Paris in a rival gallery, that of Georges Petit.

Monet worked in many places, mostly near Paris, with occasional trips to the south of France, Venice, Holland, and London. After the death of Camille he lived with the widow of his friend and patron Ernest Hoschedé; later she became his second wife. In 1890 he bought the house on the river Epte at Giverny that was his home from 1883 until his death.

There he started his famous and successful series: first, in 1890, of haystacks, which he painted at different times of day according to the changes of light; in 1891, of poplar trees; in 1893, the series of the façade of Rouen Cathedral. They sold for high prices. Monet's most remarkable works are his innumerable paintings of the water lilies in his Giverny garden and the huge horizontal canvases concerned solely with the light, color, and space of his lily-pool.

An Impressionist to the last, Monet devoted his life to observing the most transient moods of light and color. In his later work the division between reality and illusion began to disappear. His influence on his contemporaries and on the successors of Impressionism was profound, and his feeling for space, his free technique, and his bold use of color all link him with the development of 20th-century painting.

W. Seitz Claude Monet New York and London, 1960

Poplars on the Epte, 1891
London, Tate

GUSTAVE MOREAU

1826-1898

A Symbolist painter of richly wrought fantasies

Gustave Moreau was born in Paris, the son of wealthy parents. There he lived the life of a recluse, aware nevertheless of what went on around him. He also made several journeys abroad: from 1858 until 1860 to Italy, where he met Pierre Puvis de Chavannes in Rome, and in 1865 to Holland, where he studied Rembrandt.

Moreau's usual mediums were oil and watercolor; his subject matter was invariably Biblical or mythological. His style was influenced by Eugène Delacroix, and later by Théodore Chassériau and perhaps by Dante Gabriel Rossetti. Its outstanding elements are a graceful languor (Moreau's "beautiful inertia"), an opulence of detail, and a flowing arabesque line. Moreau mistrusted reason and the observation of the eye, maintaining: "Only my inward feelings seem to me eternal and incontestably certain."

Perhaps because he was by nature a perfectionist, much of his work was left unfinished. In it there is often a contradiction between the strength of the linear pattern and the heavy accumulation of detail, which increased as his style developed. In contrast, many of his color sketches are very freely handled, and when in the 1870's he experimented with modeling in wax and clay, he re-created the mythological and Biblical characters of his paintings in an animated style.

Moreau's color is rich and jewel-like. His actual obsession with jewels and fantastic detail is the closest parallel in painting to the imagery of the Symbolist poets of his time. This quality impressed the Symbolist writer and critic J. K. Huysmans, who was partly responsible for the contemporary appreciation of Moreau. Exhibited occasionally at the Paris Salon, Moreau's work appealed strongly to the "decadents" among the literary Symbolists. He was himself horrified at their private lives and had no wish to associate with them.

In the 20th century his work was later of considerable interest to the Surrealists, particularly to Max Ernst and André Breton. He was also an influential teacher, from 1892 until the year of his death, at the École des Beaux-Arts in Paris, where he had among his pupils Henri Matisse, Georges Rouault, and Matisse's friend Albert Marquet. Moreau died on April 18, 1898, leaving his collection of his own works to the state. His house in Paris is now a museum, of which Rouault was the first curator.

Oedipus and the Sphinx
Paris, Mus. Gustave Moreau

Gustave·Moreau

HIS WORKS INCLUDE
The Chimera, 1858
Paris, Mus. Gustave Moreau
Semele, about 1895
Paris, Mus. Gustave Moreau
Salome
Paris, Louvre

See also page 158

EDVARD MUNCH

1863-1944

A Norwegian painter who pioneered Expressionism and helped to revolutionize German art

Edvard Munch was born on December 12, 1863, near Løyten in southern Norway. His mother died when he was five and his elder sister when he was 14; he himself was a sickly child, and the themes of sickness and death appear frequently in his work. His father, too, was drastically affected by the mother's death, becoming subject to religious mania and varying between jocularity and insane violence.

73

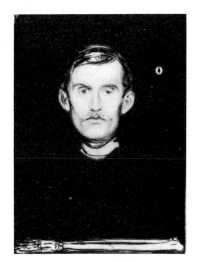

Self-portrait, 1895
Oslo, Munch-Museet, et al.

Night (detail) 1890
Oslo, Nasjonalgall.

At the age of 17 Munch entered the Oslo School of Art and Handicraft. In 1882, after two years there, he joined a group of young artists in a studio in the building where Christian Krohg, a realist painter influenced by Gustave Courbet and Édouard Manet, also worked. Although Munch's early style reflects that of Krohg, he achieved by the mid-1880's a freer and subtler handling of color and an approach to his subject unlike that of any Norwegian contemporary. The intellectual atmosphere of Oslo in the 1880's, in particular the ideas of Ibsen and Bjørnson, made a strong impact on him. Society was considered an entity to be fought and art a social weapon with which to fight it. In the first versions of paintings such as *The Day After* and *Puberty*, both of 1886, Munch used realistic observation to express social themes.

In the late 1880's Norway began to be aware of French Impressionism. In 1885 Munch had visited Paris for a few weeks. Four years afterwards he won a scholarship to Paris and was abroad until 1892. Meanwhile radical changes occurred in his style. He worked for three months at Léon Bonnat's studio in Paris, then independently. He visited the Riviera, Italy, and Germany. He saw paintings by Vincent van Gogh and Paul Gauguin in Theo van Gogh's Paris gallery. The first version of *The Yellow Boat*, 1891, contains patterns reminiscent of Gauguin. At the same time its movement into space is much stronger than anything in Gauguin.

In 1892 Munch was invited to exhibit in Berlin. This was both a key point in his own career and a significant event for Germany. His paintings caused such an outcry that the exhibition was closed in Berlin, but it went to Breslau, Dresden, and Munich, as well as Copenhagen, and pointed the direction of German Expressionism for the next few decades.

Munch had already conceived the idea of painting pictures in a cycle that he eventually called the *Frieze of Life*. Although it was never finished it occupied much of his energy. Subject matter was always important to him, and until the end of the century he was experimenting with and searching for motifs for the *Frieze of Life*. From 1892 to 1908 he returned regularly to Norway every summer. He became a friend of August Strindberg, much of whose subjective and abstract thinking he absorbed. For example the statement: "in the painter and the playwright there is a parallel preoccupation with the conflict between the sexes and other sexual problems; there is the same sense of the powerlessness of the individual in the face of love and death." To express his own experience of the dilemma of love and its consequences, Munch used a variety of styles, mediums, and motifs, with varying degrees of symbolism.

In Paris again in 1896, he concentrated on the woodcut. In this medium he made some technical innovations. For example, he was the first to make use of the wood grain and to allow his material to help dictate the form; he also evolved a new method of cutting up the blocks. Influenced by Gauguin and by Japanese prints, these woodcuts achieved a consistency of style not found in other aspects of his work.

In the early years of the 20th century Munch was recognized in Norway and achieved financial security. In 1908 in Copenhagen he suffered a nervous collapse as a result of heavy drinking and an unhappy love affair, and entered a sanatorium.

However, he continued his work there, holding a successful exhibition in Oslo. He returned to Norway in 1909 and took part the following year in a competition for decorations for Oslo University. In 1914 the commission was finally granted him. In its execution he used a simple, formal language, with many motifs close to popular visual tradition. At the Cologne Sonderbund, where he was invited to show in 1912, he was allotted, like Picasso, a whole room for his pictures.

By now nature had begun to assume a new importance for Munch. From 1910 to 1912, inspired possibly by the cinema, he experimented with the movement of figures in space. In the work of his last years he summed up his life's experience. He was obsessed both with the days of his youth and with the irony of old age; the latter is expressed in his *Between the Clock and the Bed, Self-portrait*, 1940. He died in January, 1944, having lived to see his paintings, once highly esteemed in Germany, included in the 1935 Nazi exhibition in Munich of "degenerate" art. The development of painting in central Europe and Germany, where his strongest influence on the Expressionists was in the fields of portraiture and graphic work, is indebted as much to Munch as to French art. His work was admired, in particular by Oskar Kokoschka, whose outlook has been in some ways similar.

F. B. Deknatel Munch New York, 1950
O. Benesch Edvard Munch London, 1960

HIS WORKS INCLUDE

The Artist's Sister Inger, 1884
Oslo, Nasjonalgall.

Moonlight, 1893
Oslo, Nasjonalgall.

Girls on a Jetty, 1901
Oslo, Nasjonalgall.

Summer Night at the Shore, about 1902
Vienna, Kunsthist. Mus.

The Sick Child, about 1907
London, Tate

Between the Clock and the Bed, Self-portrait, 1940
Oslo, Nasjonalgall.

See also pages 206, 207, 232

Winter, 1899
Oslo, Nasjonalgall.

CAMILLE PISSARRO

A pioneer Impressionist landscape and urban painter

The Oise near Pontoise (detail) 1876
Rotterdam, Boymans-van Beuningen

Camille Pissarro was born in St. Thomas Island in the Danish West Indies on July 10, 1830. His mother was a Creole, his father a Portuguese-Jewish store owner in St. Thomas. Pissarro went to school in Paris, returning to St. Thomas at 17 to be a clerk in his father's store. He spent all his spare time drawing, and in 1852 ran away to Venezuela with a Danish painter. His parents then decided to let him study painting in France.

He reached Paris near the end of 1855, the year of the World Exhibition there. He was thus able to see exhibitions of leading contemporary artists: Delacroix, Ingres, and Courbet; Millet, which he liked; and Corot, which he liked most of all. He went to visit Corot and was kindly received. Later he saw Corot frequently. He twice exhibited at the Paris Salon as a "pupil of Corot." But in 1866, the year in which he met Manet, they quarreled, for Corot disapproved of the influences of Manet and Courbet in Pissarro's work.

From the first Pissarro was revolutionary minded. Academic art seemed to stifle him, and he often said that the Louvre ought to be burned. He was a pupil in various studios at the École des Beaux-Arts, then attended the Atelier Suisse, where he met the young Claude Monet in 1859 and Paul Cézanne and Armand Guillaumin in 1861. He exhibited a landscape, unnoticed by the critics, at the Salon of 1859. At subsequent Salons the jury rejected his entries, but three of his landscapes were hung at the Salon des Refusés in 1863 and favorably reviewed. In 1866 his work drew praise from the writer Émile Zola. Pissarro often went to paint at the Montfoucault farm of the landscape painter Ludovic Piette, managing at the same time to keep in touch with Monet and to visit Renoir and Sisley. Before the end of 1866 he settled in Pontoise, about 20 miles from Paris.

Landscape at Chaponval, 1880
Paris, Mus. de l'Impressionnisme

The Marne, about 1865
Edinburgh, N. G. of Scotland

Now began a 30-year struggle against poverty and failure. His work, mostly landscapes done in the open air, was accepted now and then at the Salon. But by 1868 he was forced to paint blinds for a living, occasionally selling his canvases very cheaply to the dealer Père Martin. When Pissarro was in Paris he was often to be seen at the Café Guerbois, tirelessly arguing his convictions. A modest, retiring man, kindly and level-headed, he was liked and respected by the artists who met there, even by the difficult Edgar Degas.

In 1869 Pissarro took his mistress, Julie Vellay, and their growing family to Louveciennes, where he made many studies of winter landscape. During the Franco-Prussian war of 1870-71 he went first to stay with Piette in Brittany, then to London with his family. There he married Julie Vellay, and visited museums and painted London views with his fellow countryman Monet. He sold two paintings to the dealer Durand-Ruel, also a refugee in London, but when he submitted work to the Royal Academy it was rejected.

Letters from friends in France told Pissarro that the Prussians had wrecked his house at Louveciennes and trampled on his paintings. In June, 1871, he returned to Pontoise, where he was joined by Cézanne and Guillaumin. He often worked with Cézanne, and they had a considerable influence on each other. By introducing Cézanne to the paint seller Père Tanguy, he ensured for him a supply of materials in exchange for paintings.

Pissarro himself had some financial help from Durand-Ruel. In auction sales in 1873 his work fetched moderate prices. The next year he was one of the most indefatigable organizers of the first Impressionist group show. He insisted that Cézanne and Guillaumin should take part, and himself contributed five pictures. But the exhibition was greeted by the public with disdain and ridicule. In depression Pissarro left Paris for Pontoise.

The pattern of the following years was the same. He exhibited at all eight of the Impressionist group shows and worked in and around Pontoise with Cézanne or Paul Gauguin, whom he met in 1877. At other times he stayed in Brittany or Paris, where he often went to the Café de la Nouvelle-Athènes, his friends' new meeting place. With Degas and Mary Cassatt he became very interested in etching. Japanese prints fascinated him as they did Degas, though in Pissarro's case it was chiefly for the technical possibilities they suggested. Money was always scarce, but in 1878 he had help from a pastry-cook whose portrait he painted. In 1881 Durand-Ruel was again able to buy from him, and life became a little easier. The dealer gave him a one-man show in 1883, but it did not make much profit.

Dissatisfied with his own work, thinking it to be weak and formless, Pissarro moved in 1883 to Osny, not far from Pontoise, and the next year to Eragny. At the same time he made frequent trips to Paris in an effort to sell. Then Guillaumin introduced him to Paul Signac, who in turn introduced him to Georges Seurat and Pointillism. He felt he had at last found the discipline he sought, and promptly deserted Impressionism in favor of it. In 1886 he invited Seurat and Signac to exhibit with him at the eighth and final group show. The Pointillist paintings, hung in a separate room, were not understood by his friends. Pissarro showed some Pointillist canvases with Les XX in Brussels in 1887. By 1888, however, he had lost

The Bridge at Bruges, 1903
Manchester, England, City Art Gall.

The Market at Gisors, 1900
Paris, Mus. de l'Impressionnisme

faith in a style that he found too slow and labored, and in general unsuitable to his temperament. Some pictures he repainted, others he destroyed.

In 1886 he had met Vincent van Gogh, to whom he explained both Impressionism and Pointillism. While van Gogh was recovering from the series of mental crises that troubled his last years, it was hoped that he might be able to stay with Pissarro. As Mme. Pissarro was afraid of the possible effect of this on her young children, Pissarro arranged for him to be placed in the care of a friend of the Impressionists, Dr. Gachet. Pissarro admired van Gogh's work. But he could not appreciate Gauguin's mature style, feeling his production of quasi-mystical paintings to be a grave sin. It was an art in complete antithesis to his own belief in realism and socialism, though this did not prevent him from helping Gauguin when called on to do so. He also introduced Cézanne's work to the young dealer Ambroise Vollard.

Pissarro himself at last had some success. Van Gogh's brother Theo organized an exhibition of his work in Paris in 1890. In 1892 Durand-Ruel held an important Pissarro retrospective exhibition, reviewed enthusiastically by the critic Octave Mirbeau. In 1895 Pissarro, who was suffering from a severe infection of the eyes, had to give up painting out-of-doors. In his last years he made several visits to his favorite son, Lucien, also a painter, who had settled in London. In November, 1903, after a short illness, Pissarro died in Paris.

J. Rewald Camille Pissarro: Letters to his Son Lucien London, 1943
J. Rewald Camille Pissarro New York and London, 1963

Self-portrait
Paris, Petit-Palais

P. Puvis de Chavannes

PIERRE PUVIS DE CHAVANNES   1824-1898

The reviver of mural painting in France, and a source of Symbolism

Pierre Puvis de Chavannes was born on December 14, 1824, in Lyons, France, into an old Burgundian family. His father, a civil engineer, sent him to school first in Lyons, then to the Lycée Henri IV in Paris. Fascinated by science, Puvis prepared for the École Polytechnique. He also attended some lectures in law. These studies were interrupted by illness and a trip to Italy, where he was so struck by Piero della Francesca's frescoes in Arezzo that he became interested in fresco as a medium. On his return to France, Puvis resolved to become a painter.

He studied in Paris, first under Henri Scheffer and then, until 1852, under Thomas Couture, but was influenced more by Théodore Chassériau than by either of his teachers. He established himself in a studio in the Place Pigalle, where he stayed until the year before his death. Most of his large paintings were done at a studio at Neuilly in the Paris suburbs, to which he walked every day. Many of his ideas for landscape backgrounds came from looking at the Parc Monceau, whose ruined colonnade appears in *The Sacred Grove Dear to the Arts and the Muses*.

In 1850 Puvis exhibited a *Pietà* at the Salon. After 1852, however, his entries were rejected for several years by the Salon jury. When he exhibited in a private gallery the public laughed at his work, but he was defended by the writer and critic Théophile Gautier. At the Salon of 1859 Puvis showed *Return from Hunting*, and in 1861 he received a second class medal for his *Peace* and *War*. *Peace* was bought by the French government and Puvis presented *War* to the state in order that the two paintings should not be separated. They led to further commissions: decorations for the Marseilles Museum, 1865-69, which included *Ave Picardia Nutrix* and *Ludus pro Patria*; a series of paintings commemorating the historical importance of Marseilles (completed in 1869); and decorations for the town hall of Poitiers, which date from 1872 to 1875.

Puvis's work had at first reflected a variety of influences, including those of many Italian painters, but it gradually evolved toward a personal, monumental style. He felt a need to revive in huge compositions the qualities of Italian fresco painting, though he painted not in fresco but in oil on canvas. His colors were always pale and subdued, the linear element strong and simple.

The first major commission of his career was a cycle, *The Life of St. Genevieve*, for the Panthéon in Paris. These large-scale scenes were begun in 1876. In them any previous sense of three dimensionality was renounced. Puvis made decorations for the Sorbonne, from 1888 to 1889, then worked for four years on a scheme for the Paris City Hall. As soon as this was finished, in 1893, he began murals in oil on canvas for the public library in Boston, Massachusetts. They had been negotiated for since 1891 and were finished in 1895. Like the Sorbonne decorations, they were much influenced by antique art.

Puvis's independent canvases included *The Poor Fisherman* and *Hope*, copied respectively by Georges Seurat and Paul Gauguin, and *The Sacred Grove Dear to the Arts and the Muses*, which was parodied by Henri de Toulouse-Lautrec. Yet Lautrec, like Vincent van Gogh, the Nabis painters, and the sculptor Aristide Maillol, admired Puvis. They could appreciate his search, that of Symbolist art in general, for a plastic equivalent for thoughts and ideas. The literary climate of the 1880's

Young Girls by the Sea
Paris, Louvre

HIS WORKS INCLUDE
War, 1861
Amiens, Mus. de Picardie

Sleep, 1867
Lille, Pal. des B-A.

Hope, 1872
Paris, Louvre

Vision of Antiquity, about 1885
Pittsburgh, Pa., Carnegie Inst.

See also pages 159, 209

The Beheading of St. John the Baptist
London, N. G.

War, 1861
Amiens, Mus. de Picardie

was particularly sympathetic to his vision, and it was then that he enjoyed his greatest popularity. His influence touched nearly all the Paris Symbolists, as August Strindberg noticed when he came to the city in 1885. Puvis's work was still widely esteemed when he died in 1898. His wife, Princess Cantacuzène, whom he married after a long friendship, died shortly before him.

ODILON REDON   1840-1916

A Symbolist painter of visions and fantasies

Odilon Redon was born in Bordeaux, France, in 1840. A delicate child, he spent his early years on the family estate of Peyrelebade between the Médoc and Les Landes, a desolate region from whose primitive people he heard strange legends. This environment made a lasting impression on his mind and created an imaginary world for him to live in. In later years, until his family sold the estate, he went to Peyrelebade every summer to draw.

He had begun drawing at an early age. When he was 11 he was impressed by a Delacroix exhibition in Bordeaux. At the age of 15 he studied in Bordeaux with the Romantic painter Stanislas Gorin, copied engravings and English watercolors, and made careful drawings of skeletons. After unsuccessful attempts at architecture and sculpture, he enrolled in Jean Léon Gérôme's studio at the École des Beaux-Arts in Paris. However, Gérôme's different temperament and interests prevented him from learning anything there. Redon meanwhile made friends with the bota-

Portrait of Jeanne Chaise, 1903
Basel, Öffentliche Kunstsamm.

Portrait of Mademoiselle Violette Heymann, 1910
Cleveland, Ohio, Mus. of Art, Hinman B. Hurlbut Coll.

nist Armand Clavaud, with whom he examined slides under a microscope, and discussed literature—Hindu poetry, Shakespeare, Flaubert, Mallarmé—and German philosophy.

In 1863 Redon met the Bordeaux engraver Rodolphe Bresdin, to whom two years later he apprenticed himself. Bresdin's exotic engravings of forests, in which birds and flowers had almost human faces and creepers were snakes, influenced Redon's own often ambiguous forms; the engraver also introduced him to the medium of charcoal. In a review for the Bordeaux newspaper "La Gironde," Redon expressed a feeling that the *avant-garde* painters of the 1868 Paris Salon had closed their minds to spiritual aspects of art. The Franco-Prussian war of 1870-71, in which he enlisted as a private, brought him to reality and matured his outlook.

After the war he lived in Paris and worked intensively at lithography, using it until 1878 as a means of reproducing his charcoals, whose blackness was sharpened by the white paper on which they were printed. In 1879 Redon's first album of lithographs was published. Several other albums followed. In 1888, 1889, and 1896 three volumes of designs for Gustave Flaubert's "The Temptation of St. Anthony" appeared, extensions of the text rather than illustrations to it. In 1890 Redon illustrated Charles Baudelaire's "Les Fleurs du Mal." In 1891 he published ten lithographs entitled *Dreams*. His last series, *The Apocalypse*, was published in 1899 by the art dealer Ambroise Vollard.

The years between 1880 and 1885 were transitional for Redon, a time when he was admired by the Symbolist writers. He and Gustave Moreau were the only artists of the day whose concepts and work ran closely parallel with theirs. Lithographs by Redon hung in 1881 in the offices of the Paris newspaper "La Vie Moderne" and the next year in the "Gaulois" offices. They were noticed by a Symbolist writer, J. K. Huysmans, who described many of them in his novel "À Rebours" and introduced Redon to the poet Stéphane Mallarmé.

Redon exhibited in 1886, and in the following years with the group Les XX in Brussels, then with La Libre Esthétique, which replaced it. In 1886 he showed in Paris with the Impressionists. The Société des Artistes Indépendants, created by Georges Seurat, Alfred Signac, and others in 1884, made him president.

His designs alternated until 1890 between a calm and a tormented style. It was only after 1890 that painting and pastels became his fullest means of expression. Images of light and of day then began to enter his work and a mystic face was a recurring theme. After 1895 this became specifically the face of Christ. From 1900, working more from nature, Redon painted series of still-lifes and portraits. From 1905 his subjects, in brilliant colors and progressively more abstract, were generally either flowers or the chariot of Apollo. These in turn gave way after 1910 to variations on the birth of Venus.

In 1898 Vollard held an exhibition of Redon's pastels and drawings. The artist exhibited frequently in his last years, and in a variety of places: America, Russia, England, and Switzerland as well as with Vollard and other Paris dealers. Three of his pictures were hung in the 1910 London exhibition of Manet and the Post-Impressionists. At the 1913 New York Armory Show an entire section was allotted to his work.

Closed Eyes, 1890
Paris, Mus. de l'Impressionnisme

Le Regard
London, Private Coll.

Although he was an isolated figure and for the most part not appreciated in Impressionist circles, Redon himself admired a great deal of contemporary art, even that which differed radically from his own. He considered Degas the greatest of living painters, but also enjoyed Renoir's landscapes and was interested in the work of Cézanne, Seurat, Gauguin, and van Gogh. Gauguin and Émile Bernard, friends of Redon, were influenced by him.

On a visit to London in 1895 Redon saw the Elgin marbles. These classical Greek sculptures were for him the summit of all art, and, coupled with his discovery of color, turned his interest toward the art of the south. He was also fascinated by the Russian ballet and by the productions of the Paris Théâtre Libre. In 1909 and 1913 he published a memoir, "Confidences of an Artist," in two parts. In 1916 he fell ill, and died in Paris on July 6.

FRÉDÉRIC BAZILLE
Portrait of Pierre Auguste Renoir
Algiers, Mus. des B-A.

PIERRE AUGUSTE RENOIR   1841-1919

An Impressionist painter of people and the pleasures of everyday life

Pierre Auguste Renoir was born in Limoges, France, on February 25, 1841, the son of a tailor. His parents moved to Paris when he was four and apprenticed him, at 13, in a porcelain factory. When his talent for painting the prescribed designs on to pieces of porcelain ware became apparent, they were persuaded to let him attend evening art classes. He decided to become a painter.

He decorated fans and blinds and made murals in order to pay for his tuition. He managed to save a little money and in 1862 was able to enter the Paris École des Beaux-Arts. There, at Charles Gleyre's studio, he worked devotedly and made friends with his fellow students Claude Monet, Frédéric Bazille, and Alfred Sisley. Henri Fantin-Latour, who had a studio nearby, often took him to visit the Louvre. Renoir developed an admiration for the French painters of the 18th century—Boucher, Fragonard, Watteau—and never afterwards cut himself off entirely from their tradition. But he failed to find favor with his teacher, the academic Gleyre. Once, when accused of painting merely to amuse himself, he replied that he would not paint at all unless it gave him pleasure.

In 1863 Renoir went with Monet and his other friends to the Forest of Fontainebleau, the first of many visits over several years. They painted forest scenes in the villages of Chailly and nearby Marlotte. One Marlotte picture of Renoir's, *At the Inn of Mère Anthony*, 1866, is composed of a group of his friends. At Chailly he met Diaz de la Peña, a member of the Barbizon School, who gave him advice and supplies of paint and canvas.

As a young man Renoir experimented with various styles. For some forest landscapes of the mid-1860's he laid on his colors thickly with a palette-knife, rather in the manner of Gustave Courbet. Then both his handling and his palette lightened. His portrait of a young girl, *Lise*, 1867, done entirely out-of-doors, was the result of careful, first-hand observation of light and color reflected in shadows.

In the summer of 1869, while Renoir was living with Lise at his parents' house at Ville d'Avray, he worked with Monet at the bathing place of La Grenouillère, on the Seine, observing and recording the effects of light on water. For a time, his style was very close to Monet's.

By no means always satisfied with his own work, Renoir had destroyed the first painting he had had accepted, in 1864, at the Paris Salon. The public, however, always found his work more acceptable than that of any of his friends. The next year, 1865, two paintings were shown at the Salon and despite some subsequent rejections, Renoir exhibited there intermittently until 1890.

He could always find as much beauty and enjoyment in Paris as anywhere else. He sometimes spent the autumn and winter, until 1870, with Frédéric Bazille at his different Paris studios. When Monet was in town, he and Renoir painted street views together.

In July, 1870, the Franco-Prussian war began. Bazille was killed fighting in November. Renoir was drafted into a regiment of cuirassiers. He stayed in Paris during the Commune, which followed in 1871, though most of his friends were out of the city. Later in the year he painted in the suburbs. In 1872 he divided his time between Paris and visits to Monet's house at Argenteuil on the Seine. In 1873, after the sale of some canvases to the dealer Durand-Ruel, he was able to rent a studio of his own. Three years later he took a house in Montmartre.

When he was in Paris, Renoir often visited the Café Guerbois, though he rarely contributed to the discussions carried on there by the *avant garde*. He did not share the current interest in Japanese art, much preferring North African subjects as

The Swing, 1876
Paris, Mus. de l'Impressionnisme

Les Grandes Baigneuses, 1884-87
Philadelphia, Pa., Mus. of Art, Tyson Coll.

Maternity, about 1915
London, Tate, et al.

Head of a Young Girl, 1898
London, Tate

painted by Eugène Delacroix. In 1874 he took an active part in the organization of the first Impressionist group show. He was given the unenviable job of hanging the paintings, of which six were his. Unfortunately, he was ridiculed with the rest by the critic Louis Leroy.

In his Montmartre garden in 1876 Renoir asked his friends to pose for *The Swing*, and at a nearby dance-hall he painted *The Moulin de la Galette*. These two pictures, both clearly mirroring his fascination with light, were among those that he exhibited at the second group show in 1876. After the third group show the next year, he decided that he could no longer risk the notoriety involved in exhibiting with the Impressionists. He joined them in only one more show, that of 1882.

He had found several patrons in the interim, including one, Gustave Caillebotte, who left his collection of Impressionist works to the Louvre, naming Renoir his executor. Renoir met the collector Victor Chocquet in 1875, the one happy result of a financially disastrous sale of Impressionist pictures which he helped to arrange. He painted Chocquet's portrait and that of his wife, took him to see Paul Cézanne's work at Père Tanguy's shop, and introduced him to Monet. Émile Zola's publisher Georges Charpentier also became Renoir's friend and patron. A portrait of Mme. Charpentier and her children was admired at the Salon of 1879. In June of that year, Renoir held a one man show at the offices of "La Vie Moderne," a newspaper of which M. and Mme. Charpentier were founders.

Venus Victorious, 1914
London, Tate, et al.

Road Climbing through Long Grass, 1875
Paris, Mus. de l'Impressionnisme

During summers in Normandy, Chatou, or Bougival, Renoir continued for a year or two his studies of light and water. In the winter he would go south. He made two trips to Algiers and several to Spain and Italy. Visiting the Italian museums and sites for the first time in the winter of 1881, he was particularly impressed by Raphael and by the Roman frescoes at Pompeii. On his return to France he stayed for some time in L'Estaque, outside Marseilles, with Cézanne and his mother, who both nursed him with great devotion when he became ill with pneumonia.

It was after this Italian journey that, dissatisfied with the spontaneity of Impressionism, Renoir began deliberately to search for a new style and sharper outline, which was to be "a continuation of the pictures of the 18th century." Inspired by a 17th-century relief by François Girardon, he started *Les Grandes Baigneuses* in 1884. It took him three years to finish. Shown at the Petit Gallery in 1887, it was a popular success. Renoir's work began to sell. Thenceforth he exhibited frequently, amid great acclaim. Eventually he returned to a full, warm, vital style. His palette was even richer than before and dominated by the color red, of which it embraced every shade, from pale flesh tints to a deep purple.

Renoir spent his last years, from 1900 onwards, mainly in the south of France at Cagnes. In 1881 he met and later married Aline Charigot, one of the models for *The Luncheon of the Boating Party, Bougival*. His favorite model now was his wife's cousin Gabrielle, whom he had engaged as nursemaid for his children. Gradually crippled by arthritis, he nevertheless painted to the end of his life. Bent on the fullest possible expression of form, he even took up sculpture, though with the aid of an assistant. He died in Cagnes on December 3, 1919.

Gabrielle with an Open Blouse, 1907
Paris, Durand-Ruel et Cie

M. Raynal   Renoir   Geneva, 1949
W. Pach   Renoir   New York, 1951
W. Gaunt   Renoir   London, 1952
J. Renoir   Renoir, My Father   London, 1963

The Judgment of Paris, 1914
Philadelphia, Pa., coll. Henry P. McIlhenny

The Bathers, about 1918
Paris, Mus. de l'Impressionnisme

The greatest 19th-century sculptor, and the first to explore new possibilities of his medium

Auguste Rodin was born on November 12, 1840, in Paris, where his father was employed as a clerk. At the age of 14, after a period at a boarding school in Beauvais run by his uncle, Rodin entered the Petite École in Paris. His mornings were spent drawing and modeling, his afternoons at the Louvre. Twice a week he attended classes held by the animal sculptor Antoine Louis Barye. He had a remarkable natural talent and an unusual grasp of the importance of volume in sculpture.

He was three times refused admittance to the Paris École des Beaux-Arts, and set to work to earn his living as a modeler, carver, and decorator. He also spent six unsuccessful months as a novice in a monastery. In 1864 his masterly clay head, *Man with a Broken Nose*, was rejected at the Paris Salon. That year he joined the sculptor Albert Ernest Carrier-Belleuse as assistant pupil. The commercial orders on which he worked for his master included the caryatids at the Théâtre des Gobelins in Paris and decorative reliefs at the Louvre. When he was declared unfit for military service during the Franco-Prussian war of 1870-71, he accompanied Carrier-Belleuse to Belgium. He did not return to Paris until 1877, when he worked at the Sèvres porcelain factory.

Meanwhile, in 1874, he had visited Italy and succumbed to the potent influence of the sculpture and paintings of Michelangelo. They revealed to him the overriding importance of modeling and at the same time imbued him with a sense of freedom in dealing with his subject.

The Young Mother, 1885
London, Tate

The Fallen Caryatid Bearing her Stone,
about 1880   *London, Tate, et al.*

The Fallen Angel, 1895
London, Tate, et al.

When his *Age of Bronze* was shown at the Salon of 1877, he was accused of taking a cast from life. The resulting controversy, in which some sculptors and government officials sided with Rodin, ultimately brought him official patronage. Three years later the metal cast itself was purchased by the state.

In 1880 Rodin was commissioned to make a ceremonial doorway for the new Musée des Arts Décoratifs in Paris. This, *The Gates of Hell*, illustrating Dante's *Inferno* and inspired by Ghiberti's doors of the Florence Baptistery, occupied his mind for over 20 years. The commission was eventually abandoned; in fact Rodin's imagination overreached itself, and the doors became for him a repertory of his ideas. The numerous sculptured group and figures express a mixture of eroticism and despair, the idea of a flux from which life emerges. Many were later presented as individual sculptures. *Adam* and *Eve*, for example, were originally to have been placed on either side of the gate, and *The Thinker* to have surmounted it.

Rodin always met with difficulties when awarded commissions. His monument, *The Burghers of Calais*, was begun in 1884 but not erected until 1896 because of objections from the town council; the base of his monument to Claude Lorraine had to be altered; worst of all, his statue of Honoré Balzac was refused by the society that had commissioned it.

Nevertheless, Rodin's prestige continued to grow. He was invited to London in

Gustav Mahler
Paris, Mus. Rodin

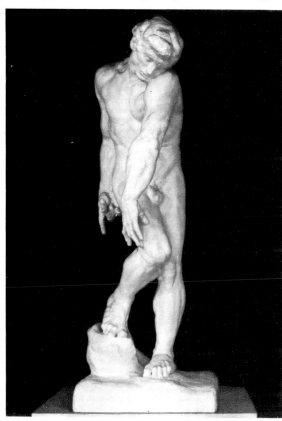

Adam, 1880
Paris, Mus. Rodin

The Burghers of Calais, begun 1884
Paris, Mus. Rodin, et al.

87

Head of Balzac, about 1892
London, Tate, et al.

1881 by his friend, Alphonse Legros the painter, etcher, and teacher. He was warmly received in England, where he afterwards came as a refugee in 1914. In 1901 he made a successful trip to Prague. When in Paris he lived in government accommodation, which consisted of a free studio from 1882, and rooms at the Hôtel Biron from 1908. Various artists and writers had been housed in the latter at state expense and, prompted by his friend Rainer Maria Rilke, the German poet, Rodin arranged to be allowed to spend the rest of his life there in exchange for the bequest of some property and all the works of art in his possession at his death. The Hôtel Biron was then to be converted into a Rodin museum, which it is today.

Rodin showed at the Brussels Exhibition in 1888, with Claude Monet in Paris in 1889, and frequently at the Paris Salons. At the 1900 International Exhibition he displayed 168 works of his own in a pavilion at the Rond-Point de l'Alma in Paris. He died at Meudon on November 17, 1917.

Rodin's position in the history of modern sculpture cannot be overestimated. No predecessor had attempted to break up surfaces, as he did, in order to give full

The Prodigal Son, about 1885
London, Tate, et al.

Brother and Sister, 1890
London, Tate, et al.

effect to the play of light. This parallel to the Impressionist idea of forms dissolved in light was encouraged in Rodin by his intensive study of ancient sculpture. He also often left parts of a carving deliberately unfinished in order to convey the idea of the figure emerging from the stone. Everything in nature, whether beautiful or ugly, interested him.

Between 1885 and 1892 his work was dominated by erotic themes inspired by his passion for Camille Claudel. His famous statue *The Kiss* dates from this time. In the later 1890's he produced a series of hands that are linked in feeling with the Symbolist movement. These were followed by a number of symbolic female figures in marble and male portraits in bronze, from which Jacob Epstein later learned a great deal. Rodin's last years were devoted to his drawings, which were often in pencil and wash and always closely connected with his sculpture. He was particularly concerned in both mediums with the expression of movement.

J. Cladel Rodin New York, 1951
A. Elsen Rodin New York, 1964

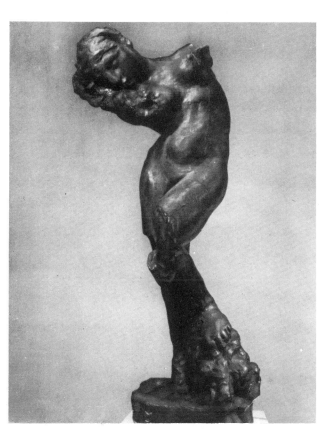

The Muse, about 1897
London, Tate

The Kiss, 1901-4 (later version)
London, Tate

Self-portrait, 1861
Birmingham, England, City Art Gall.

Poet, painter, and founder member of the Pre-Raphaelite Brotherhood

Dante Gabriel Rossetti was born in London in 1828, where his Italian father, a patriot, poet, and Dante scholar, had been living for four years in political exile. The young Rossetti steeped himself from early childhood in romantic literature, wrote poetry, and at 17 began translating Dante. He was taught drawing by John Sell Cotman, in London, and at Sass's Academy and the Royal Academy Antique School. In 1848 he begged Ford Madox Brown to accept him as a pupil, but with no master was he patient enough to learn perspective or the technicalities of rendering "pickle jars." About this time he met William Holman Hunt and John Everett Millais, and the three were one in their reaction against Victorian materialism and conventions of painting. From engravings of early Italian masters they saw the simplicity of art before Raphael, and they named themselves the Pre-Raphaelite Brotherhood. In 1849 the first picture to be signed P.R.B. appeared. The painting was Rossetti's *The Girlhood of Mary Virgin* for which his sister Christina, the poetess, sat. It accorded with the Brotherhood's ideal of expressing high moral or social ideas painted realistically from nature and individual models.

The Brotherhood did not last long, however, perhaps because each member had his own version of the ideal. In 1850 the Pre-Raphaelites were ferociously attacked in the English press by the novelist Charles Dickens and others. Rossetti, deeply sensitive to criticism, stopped exhibiting.

He painted no longer in the agreed Pre-Raphaelite manner, but filled his pictures with imaginatively, not scientifically observed detail, and idealized his subjects. His themes were the literary ones of medieval romance. His only socially conscious picture, *Found*, was worked at intermittently for 29 years and left unfinished at his death.

The Wedding of St. George and Princess Sabra,
about 1857   *London, Tate*

Dante's Dream, 1869-71
Liverpool, England, Walker Art Gall.

The 1850's were Rossetti's best years. In 1850 he met Elizabeth Siddall, who became his favorite model and sat for his paintings of Beatrice, Dante's love. About 1853 he changed the order of his Christian names (Gabriel Charles Dante) to Dante Gabriel. He used watercolors in a new way, very dry, like oils, and in bright, contrasting shades.

The artist and critic John Ruskin was now championing the Pre-Raphaelites in the press, and until 1861 was Rossetti's generous if exacting patron. Edward Coley Burne-Jones came to London to learn from Rossetti in 1856 and introduced him to William Morris, Arthur Hughes, and others at Oxford. They all undertook distemper decorations on the outside walls of the Oxford Union, but as they knew nothing of fresco techniques their paintings disintegrated almost at once.

Rossetti's association with the consumptive, enigmatic Elizabeth Siddall was stormy and tortured. He did not marry her until 1860; in 1862 she died from an overdose of laudanum. Overcome with remorse, Rossetti buried his poems with her, and then produced his final Beatrix, the *Beata Beatrix*, as a memento of her. At this time his popularity as a painter was growing, but he tended to produce somewhat repetitive voluptuous single female figures.

Living in London, in Cheyne Walk on the river Thames, he collected the blue Oriental china that later, through him and his friend James McNeill Whistler, became a vogue. In 1869, after much indecision, he had his poems disinterred and published. They were well received in both England and America, and Rossetti was active as a poet until his death. From 1869 to 1871 he painted his last important picture, *Dante's Dream*.

In 1871, a savage and unjust indictment of Rossetti's motives as a poet was published. This article, and his constant use of drugs in his last years, undermined his health. He died in Birchington, Kent, a virtual recluse, on April 9, 1882.

His work left its mark on William Morris's Arts and Crafts movement, and also influenced the Symbolist painters, including Moreau and Redon in France. Rossetti can be regarded as a precursor of Art Nouveau. The magazine "The Studio," which first appeared in 1893, carried his designs all over Europe.

H. C. Marillier   D. G. Rossetti   London, 1899
H. R. Angeli   D. G. Rossetti   London, 1949
O. Doughty   A Victorian Romantic, D. G. Rossetti   London, 1949
R. Glynn Grylls   Portrait of Rossetti   London, 1965

Mary Magdalene, 1878
London, Tate

MEDARDO ROSSO   1858-1928

An Italian who brought Impressionism to sculpture

Medardo Rosso was born in Turin, Italy, in 1858, the son of the city stationmaster. Later his family moved to Milan. As a child Rosso played truant from school to visit a monument mason who taught him to handle a chisel and hammer. This distressed and angered his parents. At the age of 23, after a period of military service as unsatisfactory as his home life, he enrolled at the Brera Academy in Milan,

Ecce Puer, 1906
Rome, Gall. Naz. d'Arte Moderna

where he learned to draw classical statues and copy them in gesso. But academic art appeared to him entirely artificial, unrelated to the world around him. Before long he helped to organize the Brera students into demanding life models for the drawing classes. As a result of his revolutionary behavior he was expelled from the school. He moved to Rome, where he lived in great poverty, sleeping among the ruins of the Colosseum.

To the end of his life Rosso battled unremittingly against the academicians. What absorbed, even obsessed, him was the problem of interpreting life itself. In 1882, some time before he saw any Impressionist paintings, he produced his fully impressionistic sculptures, *The Street Singer* and *Lovers under the Lamplight*. In 1884 some friends arranged an exhibition for him in Paris, where he lived for a time in a cheap boarding-house. He also showed that year in Paris at the newly founded Salon des Indépendants. He met Edgar Degas and called on Auguste Rodin, who was interested in and indeed not uninfluenced by him. The sculptor and teacher Jules Dalou allowed him to work in his Paris studio.

In 1885 Rosso returned to Milan, but he never lost contact with Paris. During an open competition held in Milan for a funeral monument to the critic Filippo Filippi, Rosso, who had quickly finished his entry, set it up on the grave without waiting for the judges to announce their decision. On this occasion there was a great outcry against him, but by continuing to follow these tactics in galleries and exhibitions, he gradually wore down the resistance of the authorities.

In 1886 the writer Émile Zola bought a bronze by Rosso, who thereby gained a measure of celebrity. Auguste Rodin offered to exchange a torso of his own for Rosso's recent head of a laughing woman. Rosso's work, praised also by Degas, always enjoyed greater esteem in France than in Italy. Nevertheless he had some influence on Italian painting and made a powerful impact on Italian sculpture, which had remained virtually static since the time of the Neoclassical Antonio Canova. His admirers have included the Futurists Carlo Carrà and Umberto Boccioni, and the modern Milanese sculptors Giacomo Manzu and Marino Marini.

Rosso came closer, however, than any other sculptor has to the methods of the Impressionist painters. It was his constant concern to translate into solid sculpture the transitory effects of light. So by means of rough, spontaneous modeling he manipulated light and shade in such a way as almost to produce the effect of color. In this process the distinctive characteristics of his material played an increasingly important part. Indeed, his sense of the necessity for truth to materials became one of the ideals of 20th-century art.

Rosso was able to maintain a studio in Paris and to hold a number of exhibitions. In 1896 he showed in London at the Goupil Gallery. He also had a success in New York. Toward the end of his life he suffered from diabetes and a malignant growth on the foot. He made few sculptures after 1900. He died on March 31, 1928, after the amputation of the affected leg.

HIS WORKS INCLUDE

Impressions in the Omnibus, 1882
Rome, Gall. Naz. d'Arte Moderna

Laughing Woman, 1890
Paris, Mus. Rodin

The Sick Child, 1892
Dresden, Albertinum

A Bookmaker, 1894
New York, Mus. of Modern Art

See also pages 254, 255

HENRI ROUSSEAU, called THE DOUANIER   1844-1910

The first and greatest of the naive, or primitive, painters

Henri Rousseau was born in 1844 in Laval in northern France. At the age of 18 he was conscripted into the French army and served as a musician in a military band. On his release four years later he became a clerk, returning to the army as a non-commissioned officer during the Franco-Prussian war, 1870-71. He worked in the Paris customs service for some years, thus acquiring his nickname the Douanier, the Customs Official. Moved by the simple desire for self-expression, he started painting in his spare time. In 1885 he retired on a small pension, which he supplemented by teaching drawing and the violin. At last he was able to paint full time. The next year he began exhibiting at the Salon des Indépendants.

Rousseau's first dated work, *The Small Mill*, 1880, shows both his fascination with detail and concern for the simplification of forms. At first, for example, he painted exclusively front views. These qualities were even more apparent ten years later in *Myself, Portrait Landscape*, 1890, with its seeming simplicity and, in contrast, its structural sophistication and strong surface pattern. In this as in his other portraits Rousseau took pains to choose the landscape background appropriate to the sitter. He wished his compositions to look as "real" as he could make them. His *Storm in the Jungle*, 1891, was not only the first manifestation in his work of a feeling for movement, but also the first of many jungle scenes, for which he went to the zoo to make sketches. He enlarged garden plants to take the place of bushes and trees.

It was *The Hungry Lion*, shown in Paris at the Salon d'Automne of 1905, that gave Rousseau a name for being *avant-garde*. Picasso, whom he met in 1906, André Derain, Robert Delaunay, and other young artists now became interested in him.

Myself, Portrait Landscape, 1890
Prague, Národni Gal.

In the Forest, about 1886
Zurich, Kunsthaus

Jungle Scenery with Setting Sun
Basel, Öffentliche Kunstsamm.

93

Flowers, about 1910
London, Tate

In 1907 Mme. Delaunay commissioned *The Snake Charmer*, one of his best works. The next year Picasso held a very gay, somewhat noisy banquet in his Montmartre studio for the quiet, elderly Rousseau.

Rousseau himself was conscious from the first of a need to be modern, introducing airplanes, balloons, and the Eiffel Tower into his paintings, and making many views of Paris and its suburbs. The portrait of *Pierre Loti*, 1891, a composition in the manner of the 15th-century Hans Memling, exemplifies Rousseau's interest in museum art in general and medieval painting in particular, though he "never remembered the names." However, even this portrait was brought up to date with factory chimneys and a cigarette. To Picasso he remarked: "Picasso, you and I are the greatest painters of our time, you in the Egyptian style, I in the modern."

Georges Braque and Ferdinand Léger, as well as Picasso, were influenced by Rousseau. *The Sleeping Gypsy*, one of his most influential works, was painted as early as 1897. Not only did its dreamlike quality and unexpected juxtapositions foreshadow Surrealism, but its distortions and depth-suggesting asymmetries also anticipated certain Cubist still-lifes. The guitar, seen here by the side of the sleeping figure, reappeared in many Cubist paintings. Some of Rousseau's late work was in its turn affected by his own admiration for Picasso.

The Customs House, about 1900
London, Courtauld Inst. Gall.

The Snake Charmer, 1907
Paris, Mus. de l'Impressionnisme

94

The last four years of his life were among his most productive. The dealers Uhde and Ambroise Vollard were buying part of his output, but he never accumulated a fortune. In 1908 and 1909 he held musical soirées in his studio, at which his neighbors mixed in large numbers with his *avant-garde* friends. He died in Paris on September 4, 1910.

D. C. Rich   Henri Rousseau   New York, 1942
J. Bouret   Henri Rousseau   London, 1962

HIS WORKS INCLUDE

Portrait of Pierre Loti, 1891
Zurich, Kunsthaus
The Sleeping Gypsy, 1897
New York, Mus. of Modern Art
The Snake Charmer, 1907
Paris, Mus. de l'Impressionnisme
The Dream, 1910
New York, Mus. of Modern Art

See also pages 182, 183

The Waterfall, 1910
Chicago, Art Inst., Helen Birch Bartlett Memorial Coll.

ALBERT PINKHAM RYDER   1847-1917

An imaginative painter, the most original of his generation in America

The sea was as important an element in Albert Pinkham Ryder's life as it was in Winslow Homer's. Ryder was born in the whaling port of New Bedford, Massachusetts, on March 19, 1847. There he lived until he was 22, when his family moved to New York. Having shown an aptitude for drawing at an early date, he studied in New York under William E. Marshall, a portraitist, engraver, and former pupil of the French painter Thomas Couture. At 24 Ryder entered the American National Academy of Design.

After he had finished his studies he lived a quiet, solitary life in New York,

HIS WORKS INCLUDE

The Dead Bird
Washington, D. C., Phillips Coll.
Siegfried and the Rhine Maidens
1875-91
Washington, D. C., N. G.
The Race Track, 1888-1910
Cleveland, Ohio, Mus. of Art

See also page 200

Self-portrait (detail)
Detroit, Mich., coll. Mr and Mrs.
L. A. Fleischman

The Temple of the Mind, before 1888
Buffalo, N. Y.
Albright Knox Art Gall.

creating out of his imagination and his dreams an intense, visionary art that contained not the smallest reflection of the city life around him. Even the paintings based most closely on nature exhale a sense of mystery. Nor was Ryder a literary painter, though literary sources provided titles for many of his works. His scenes from Shakespeare and the Wagnerian cycles are deeply subjective interpretations of old stories. In them, as in all his works, the design is coherent and the pictorial harmony strong.

In his 70 years Ryder traveled very little apart from rare trips to Europe: a month in London in 1877; an English tour five years later with his friend the art dealer Daniel Cottier; and a journey to France, Holland, Italy, Spain, and Tangier with the sculptor Olin L. Warner. Ryder took little notice of the contents of European galleries, glancing cursorily at the old masters and paying little attention to contemporary trends. More to his taste were the two Atlantic crossings that he made with a sea captain friend, and the nights that he spent on deck observing the sky and the sea. Walks at night in New York provided many of the strange backgrounds and stormy skies that appear in his paintings.

Perhaps it is true to say that the work of Washington Allston, the first American painter to evolve for himself an artistic vocabulary for the expression of an independent, personal vision, was to some extent the precedent Ryder followed. Ryder himself had no followers, but his work was not so much akin to the Romanticism of the 19th century as to the new plastic freedom of the 20th.

He never dated his paintings. He would often work on one for years. Thus their total number, about 160, is small, and few are on a sizeable scale or even finished. In any case Ryder matured slowly, so that the first exhibition of his works, in 1873, did not attract much attention. He was a founder of the Society of American Artists. This was the most *avant-garde* institution in America at the time, and for about 20 years the opponent and rival of the National Academy of Design. The two societies merged in 1906. During the 1880's Ryder exhibited with both, but he

Siegfried and the Rhine Maidens, 1875-91
Washington, D. C., N. G.

Gay Head
Washington, D. C., Phillips Coll.

did not become an associate of the Academy until 1902, nor an Academician until 1906. Meanwhile, his friend Cottier interested collectors in his work.

After about 1900 Ryder's output almost ceased; most of his time was spent in reworking old pictures, many of which had already deteriorated as a result of his unsound techniques. By now, however, he was in demand. He was included in the New York Armory Show of 1913, at which much *avant-garde* European art was displayed. Two years later he became chronically ill, and died on Long Island on March 28, 1917.

L. Goodrich   Albert P. Ryder   New York, 1959

Ryder

JOHN SINGER SARGENT   1856-1925

A cosmopolitan painter of brilliant, fashionable portraits

John Singer Sargent was born in Florence, Italy, in 1856, the son of wealthy expatriate Americans. His first art lessons took place in Florence, but the family traveled around Europe for some years and finally settled in Paris in 1874.

On a trip to Venice, Sargent had met and been encouraged by James McNeill Whistler. He joined the Paris École des Beaux-Arts, entering the studio of Carolus-Duran, an unimaginative but technically dexterous painter, exact in the formal organization of his subject matter. Sargent was precocious and took full advantage of the thoroughness of his training. In 1877 he exhibited a portrait at the Paris Salon. He spent a few months in Spain in 1879, as a result of which he adopted Velázquez' rich coloring on pale contrasting backgrounds. Of the work of contemporary artists, Manet's paintings most attracted him.

Sargent's style matured quickly. His sparkling portraits, so full of virtuosity as to

Self-portrait
Florence, Uffizi

Carnation, Lily, Lily, Rose, 1885-86
London, Tate

Portrait of Vernon Lee, 1881
London, Tate

HIS WORKS INCLUDE
The Luxembourg Gardens
in Twilight, 1879
Minneapolis, Minn., Mus. of Art
Miss Ellen Terry as Lady Macbeth
1889
London, Tate
Portrait of Graham Robertson, 1894
London, Tate
Sir Philip Sassoon, 1923
London, Tate

See also page 191

97

Madame X (Madame Gautreau) 1884
New York, Met. Mus.

be almost facile, mirror his cosmopolitan background and easy acquaintance with society. He won notoriety at the Salon of 1884, with his portrait of Mme. Gautreau, a Parisian beauty and society woman. The public, the sitter, her family, and the critics reacted violently to the painting, with condemnation of the "shocking" décolletage. Sargent was startled and bitterly upset. The next year he moved to London, his home for the rest of his life, and in 1887 caused a pleasant stir at the Royal Academy with his *Carnation, Lily, Lily, Rose*, in which an exotic Japanese influence was much in evidence. He often went to America. His first show there was held in January, 1888. In 1893 he exhibited nine pictures at the Chicago World Fair. In 1909 he was commissioned to decorate a room in the new Public Library in Boston, Massachusetts. The resulting murals, warm, rich, and monumental, depicted the history of the Jewish and Christian religions and were the subject of continual controversy.

Sargent's decorations, 1916-25, for the dome of the Boston Museum of Fine Arts are of a very different type, light and airy. His color grew paler in these later years and, although his brushwork never lost its liveliness and fluidity, his technique became repetitive. Any earlier sense of urgency was gone.

From about 1910 Sargent worked a great deal in watercolor, producing landscapes full of vibrant light and far more spontaneous than his portraits ever were. Nevertheless his most interesting painting is perhaps his *Portrait of Robert Louis Stevenson*. It is unusual to an extent that perturbed Stevenson himself. The writer is seen to one side of the composition, pacing a room; a hall opens out in the background, and to the right there is a glimpse of Mrs. Stevenson in an Indian costume.

Sargent died in London in April, 1925, having been for many years lionized as a fashionable portraitist. Although he made no real contribution to the development of painting, he appealed to an Edwardian public that delighted in his obvious enjoyment of rich surfaces and the vitality he gave to the features of his sitters.

C. M. Mount   John Singer Sargent, a Biography   New York, 1955

GIOVANNI SEGANTINI   1858-1899

A largely self-taught painter of mountain scenery

Giovanni Segantini was born at Arco near Lake Garda, Italy, an Italian by blood but an Austrian by nationality. As a child he was delicate, imaginative, much influenced by his early surroundings. When he was five his mother died and his father, a carpenter, took him to Milan, finally leaving him in the care of a half-sister. After two years of loneliness he ran away, intending to go to France.

He was found and brought up by peasants in the Italian Alps but eventually returned to Milan, where he studied ornamental drawing at the evening school of the Brera Academy. Hardly able to maintain himself, however, he had to be put into a reformatory. There he remained for several years. He was allowed to do a certain amount of drawing, and came to work for a painter of religious banners, returning to the Brera Academy for lessons in figure drawing. In 1879 Segantini did his first oil painting, *The Choir of the Church of S. Antonio*. In it he used a technique, similar to Pointillism or Neo-Impressionism, that he had developed, apparently, simply by means of observing light and color at first hand.

After spending a few years in Milan painting *genre* subjects, Segantini moved to the Lake Como district with his young wife. The rest of his life was spent in virtual isolation as he moved higher and higher into the Alps. He was not an influential painter. Although he exhibited in his later years in various European cities, he hardly ever left the mountains and never went farther than Milan.

Segantini's subject-matter was little influenced by any outside art, but after he had seen reproductions of the Dutch painter Anton Mauve, a relative and teacher of Vincent van Gogh, his style broadened and became more luminous. He worked out-of-doors and, like the Neo-Impressionists, experimented with optical mixtures, or the blending of color not on the canvas but in the eye of the beholder. For some years the subjects of Segantini's oils and drawings were the life of the peasants around him, the mother-child relationship, and the Alpine scenery. He also produced, throughout his life, remarkably penetrating portraits.

Suddenly he developed a symbolist style and subject-matter, nurtured in him by the various influences of the writer Zola, the philosopher Nietzsche, the composer Wagner, and the German Romantic painters. Even his symbolist pictures had mountain backgrounds. His last, unfinished, work was an elaborate triptych called *Life, Nature, and Death* and set in the familiar Alpine landscape. While climbing the Schafberg, in the course of painting this picture, he caught a chill, developed peritonitis, and died on September 28, 1899.

HIS WORKS INCLUDE

At the Watering Trough, 1888
Basel, Öffentliche Kunstsamm.

The Dead Kid, 1892
Saint Moritz, Segantini Mus.

Love at the Fount of Life, 1896
Milan, Gall. d'Arte Moderna

Springtime, 1896
Milan, Brera

Triptych: Life, Nature, and Death, about 1899 (unfinished)
Saint Moritz, Segantini Mus.

See also page 201

An Idyll
Aberdeen, Scotland, Mus.

The Punishment of Luxury, 1891
Liverpool, England, Walker Art Gall.

GEORGES SEURAT

GEORGES SEURAT (photo)

A painter and color theorist who developed the scientific style known as Neo-Impressionism

Georges Seurat was born in 1859 in Paris, where he became a pupil at the École des Beaux-Arts. As a student, he read Eugène Chevreul's books on color theory, first published over 30 years before Seurat was born. He also made an intensive study of the work of Eugène Delacroix, absorbing from the "Diaries" Delacroix's tentative theories on color. Out of this reading he evolved a precise system of his own, of which the basic principle was that colors should be allowed to mix to the required effect in the eye of the beholder, producing what are known as optical mixtures. Local color, light, and shade were therefore to be broken down by the painter into tiny, contrasting, complementary colored patches.

Seurat was stimulated by the paintings and drawings of Corot, Millet, and the Impressionists Monet and Pissarro. He felt, however, that these painters applied their ideas too hesitantly, that color was in fact controlled by fixed laws which could be learned.

Having spent the year 1880 in military service at Brest on the coast of Brittany, he devoted two years to working exclusively in black and white. He mastered the most subtle nuances of contrast and gradation of tone, until he could determine, in black and white, the exact degree of tone necessary. In 1883 a portrait drawing was accepted for the Paris Salon. At the same time, carefully following the theories that

HIS WORKS INCLUDE

Une Baignade, about 1884
London, N. G.

Les Poseuses, about 1888
Merion, Pa., Barnes Foundation

The Parade, 1888
New York, Met. Mus.

A Fishing Fleet at Port-en-Bessin, 1888
New York, Met. Mus.

Le Chahut, 1890
Otterlo, Holland, Kröller-Müller

Woman Powdering Herself, 1891
London, Courtauld Inst. Gall.

The Circus, 1891
Paris, Mus. de l'Impressionnisme

See also pages 162, 163, 164, 165, 224, 225

Le Bec du Hoc, Grandcamp, 1885
London, Tate

he had begun to formulate and was continually refining, Seurat worked on his first large composition, *Une Baignade*, almost seven by ten feet in size.

Early in 1884 he exhibited a study for this at the Paris Cercle des Arts Libéraux. The finished painting was rejected, however, by the Salon jury of 1884 and shown instead that summer at the newly formed Salon des Indépendants, of which Seurat was a founder member. Paul Signac was another. These two painters exerted a mutual influence from the moment they met. Signac persuaded Seurat to use only pure colors, and himself adopted Seurat's scientific methods.

That year, 1884, Seurat, who was as concerned with surface pattern as with coloring, made on-the-spot studies, painted on small panels of wood, of the landscape and people of the island of La Grand Jatte on the Seine near Paris. The final composition, *A Sunday Afternoon on the Island of La Grande Jatte*, as big as *Une Baignade*, occupied him until March of the next year, covering the canvas with small dots of color. At Grandcamp on the English Channel in the summer of 1885, he painted several seascapes in the same technique, including one of a large rock, *Le Bec du Hoc, Grandcamp*. In following summers he visited other Channel resorts, such as Honfleur and Port-en-Bessin.

The new style was variously called Neo-Impressionism, Pointillism, and Divisionism. Pissarro was so struck by it, when he met Seurat, that he threw himself wholeheartedly into the practice of it. He invited Seurat and Signac to share in the eighth, and last, Impressionist group show, in Paris in 1886. On this occasion

The Seine at Courbevoie, about 1887
Brussels, Mus. Royaux des B-A.

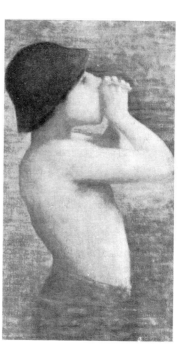

Une Baignade (detail) about 1884
London, N. G.

A Sunday Afternoon on the Island of
La Grande Jatte (detail) about 1885
*Chicago, Art Inst., Helen Birch Bartlett
Memorial Coll.*

people were doubled up with laughter in front of *La Grande Jatte*, and the other exhibiting artists were equally uncomprehending. However, the Salon des Indépendants of the same year, in which Seurat and Signac, Pissarro and his son, Lucien Pissarro, all took part, was reviewed for "L'Art Moderne" by the journalist Félix Fénéon, an admirer and spokesman of Neo-Impressionism. Seurat also became an intimate friend of the scientist and mathematician Charles Henry, whose theories on the symbolism of numbers and of color fascinated him.

In February, 1887, eight paintings by Seurat, including *La Grande Jatte* and *Le Bec du Hoc, Grandcamp*, caused great excitement at the Société des XX in Brussels. Meanwhile the dealer Durand-Ruel had sent *Une Baignade* on exhibition to New York. In Paris in 1887 Seurat showed in the lobby of the Théâtre Libre with Signac and Vincent van Gogh. Van Gogh was impressed and influenced by Pointillism without ever binding himself to its rules. For several years Seurat contributed drawings to the periodical "La Vie Moderne." He continued to show with the Indépendants in Paris and with Les XX in Brussels.

In *La Parade*, which he began in the autumn in 1887, the effect on him of Henry's theories became apparent. As later in *Le Chahut* and in his last, unfinished painting, *The Circus*, the lighting was artificial rather than natural, and design gradually predominated over color. Henry's connections with the contemporary

Woman Powdering Herself, 1891
London, Courtauld Inst. Gall.

Le Chahut, 1890
Otterlo, Holland, Kröller-Müller

Symbolist literature were reflected in Seurat's growing concern with the meaning implicit in certain lines and patterns.

Toward the end of his life Seurat began to feel that his followers and admirers were plagiarizing his ideas. Suspicion and jealousy colored his dealings with his friends. In 1888 an article appeared in which the author castigated Seurat's "unscrupulous comrades" for helping themselves to his ideas. Signac believed that Seurat himself lay behind this and wrote to him at once. The reply was not reassuring. In 1890 Seurat wrote out for a friend a summary of his theories, probably intending to emphasize his own leadership of the Neo-Impressionist movement.

About this time many of his followers defected. Pissarro, disillusioned with Pointillism, returned in 1888 to the Impressionist camp. In 1891 Seurat suddenly became ill. Two days later he died in Paris, on March 29, at the age of 32. Although Neo-Impressionism as a movement flourished only intermittently, he had made a very individual contribution to the development of modern painting.

The Lighthouse, Honfleur
Location unknown

J. Rewald Georges Seurat New York, 1946
H. Dorra and J. Rewald Seurat Paris, 1959

La Parade (detail) 1889
New York, Met. Mus.

Off to the Pub, about 1916
London, Tate

HIS WORKS INCLUDE

Café des Tribunaux, Dieppe, 1898
London, Tate

Victor Lecour, 1924
Manchester, England, City Art Gall.

Sir Thomas Beecham Conducting, about 1935
New York, Mus. of Modern Art

See also pages 193, 240

WALTER RICHARD SICKERT 1860-1942

A cosmopolitan Impressionist painter who captured the flavor of town life

Walter Sickert was born in Munich on May 31, 1860. His mother was an English-woman, his father a Danish artist employed in Germany as an illustrator on a comic journal. In 1868 the family settled in England. When Sickert left school at the age of 17 he wished to paint but, discouraged from this by his father, turned instead to the stage. In 1881, however, after four years of small parts under Henry Irving and other well known actors, he entered the Slade Art School in London.

At about this time he met James McNeill Whistler, and became his studio assistant in 1882. The next year, armed with letters of introduction to Manet and Degas, he was entrusted with seeing Whistler's *Portrait of the Artist's Mother* safely to Paris, where it was to be shown at the Salon. Manet was ill, but Degas received the young painter, and their friendship lasted until Degas's death in 1917.

As was to be expected, Sickert's early work, influenced by Whistler and Degas and concerned, like theirs, with form and composition rather than color and light, was as untypical of Impressionism as theirs. When Sickert showed for the first time, at the Society of British Artists in London, in 1884, it was as a "pupil of Whistler."

His life slipped into a regular pattern, unbroken for 15 years. In 1885 he married the daughter of a Liberal politician and spent the summer, like many subsequent summers, across the English Channel in Dieppe. He also visited Venice from time to time. He made numerous paintings from his sketches of the London

Ennui, about 1913
London, Tate

St. Mark's Square, Venice, about 1903
Newcastle-upon-Tyne, England, Laing Art Gall.

104

music halls and their audiences, or held evening classes. In 1893 he opened an art school in London under Whistler's patronage. He often showed with the New English Art Club, founded in 1886 in opposition to the Royal Academy. He showed once with Les XX in Brussels and took part in the exhibition of British Impressionists held in London in 1889. In 1894 and 1895 his paintings were reproduced in "The Yellow Book," to which Aubrey Beardsley was the chief contributor at the time.

Sickert's friendship with the dictatorial Whistler ended after a court case in which they took opposite sides. In 1899 Sickert was divorced and went to live in Venice, Dieppe, and Paris for six years. Back in London in 1905, he set up a studio in Soho and took rooms in Camden Town. His output was now almost exclusively music hall scenes and the faded life around him. He taught at the Westminster Institute, started a school for etching, and held shows at London and Paris galleries.

In 1911 Sickert founded the Camden Town Group, enlarged and renamed the London Group three years later. Among the original members were Lucien Pissarro and Spencer Gore (who were exponents of the Neo-Impressionist, or Pointillist style that Sickert adopted for a time), Augustus John, and Henry Lamb, all of whom were accustomed to meet in his studio. Among the members of the enlarged group were Jacob Epstein and Paul and John Nash.

Sickert became an associate of the Royal Academy in 1924 and an academician ten years later. But shortly afterwards he resigned in protest against the hostile attitude of the president toward the work of Epstein. In 1941 Sickert was honored with a one-man exhibition at the National Gallery in London. The next year he died in Bath, England, on January 22.

Much of his later career was devoted to teaching and writing. The merit of his later paintings, which were frequently re-creations of press photographs or Victorian illustrations, is hotly contested. They have been regarded both as a deplorable lapse in quality and as Sickert's most interesting work.

O. Sitwell A Free House, being the writings of Walter Richard Sickert London, 1947
L. Browse Sickert London, 1960

Portrait of Aubrey Vincent Beardsley
1894
London, Tate

PAUL SIGNAC   1863-1935

The propagandist of Neo-Impressionism

Paul Signac was born in Paris in 1863 and became an early admirer of Monet. He painted in Paris with his friend Armand Guillaumin, an artist on the fringe of Impressionism. In 1884 he met Monet himself, and Georges Seurat.

As a result of discussions with Seurat, Signac was suddenly drawn away from Impressionism by the pursuit of the Divisionist style of painting, which consisted in the use of small dots of color, intended to combine and blend not on the canvas but in the viewer's eye. An early example, Seurat's *Une Baignade*, was exhibited in

The Harbor at Saint-Tropez, 1893
Wuppertal, Germany, Städtisches Mus.

the summer of 1884 at the Paris Salon des Indépendants, of which he and Seurat were both founder members. Signac was tireless in his attempts to convert others to Seurat's methods. In 1886, for instance, he noticed some Divisionist paintings by Émile Bernard and went to visit him, hoping to enlist another disciple for Seurat. But he succeeded only in alienating Bernard, who became a violent opponent both of Signac and of Divisionism.

In 1885 Signac met Camille Pissarro, whom he introduced to Seurat. Pissarro had reached a crucial point of his artistic development. Finding in Seurat's technique the answer to his craving for a rational style, he adopted it with enthusiasm. Against the wishes of the Impressionists, he invited the Pointillists to participate in their eighth and last group show in 1886. On this occasion Signac exhibited mostly scenes of the Breton port of Saint-Briac and of the Paris suburbs. A big canvas, *Two Milliners*, 1885, was the first example of the application of the Divisionist technique (also called Neo-Impressionist and Pointillist) to an indoor subject.

Many of Signac's paintings are of the French coast. He left the capital each summer, to stay in the south of France in the village of Collioure or at St. Tropez, where he bought a house and invited his friends. In March, 1889, he visited Vincent van Gogh at Arles. The next year he made a short trip to Italy, seeing Genoa, Florence, and Naples.

His friends included the journalist Félix Fénéon and the scientist and mathe-

P. Signac

Still-life (Soleil) 1883
West Berlin, Staatl. Mus.

matician Charles Henry, both of whom were interested in Neo-Impressionism and published their views on color theory. In 1890 Fénéon devoted an issue of "Les Hommes d'Aujourd'hui" to the work of Signac. In the same year the artist painted a picture entitled *Against the Enamel of a Background Rhythmic with Beats and Angles, Tones and Colors*, and a *Portrait of Félix Fénéon*. The abstract patterning of the background had some part in the development of Symbolism.

Signac contributed annually to the Salon des Indépendants. He was the first non-Belgian member of the *avant-garde* Brussels Société des XX, with which he showed for some years. In Brussels in 1889, he supported Toulouse-Lautrec in his quarrel with a minor Belgian painter who had insulted Vincent van Gogh. With Seurat and van Gogh, Signac exhibited in Paris in 1887 at the Théâtre Libre.

After Seurat's death in 1891, he helped to list and classify his work. The leadership of the Neo-Impressionist movement, he felt, rested now with himself. In 1892 he took part in a Neo-Impressionist group show. Among many exhibitions that he helped to organize were memorial shows for van Gogh and Seurat, in 1891 and 1892 respectively. In 1899 Signac published a book under the title "From Eugène Delacroix to Neo-Impressionism," a summary of the ideas and theories of the movement.

HIS WORKS INCLUDE

Two Milliners, 1885
Zurich, Bührle Coll.

Passage du Puits Bertin, Clichy, 1886
New York, Met. Mus.

Le Déjeuner, about 1887
Otterlo, Holland, Kröller-Müller

Pier at Port-Rieux, 1888
Otterlo, Holland, Kröller-Müller

Portrait of Félix Fénéon, 1890
Zurich, Bührle Coll.

Le Château des Papes, Avignon, 1900
Paris, Mus. d'Art Moderne

Le Pont des Arts, 1928
Paris, Petit-Palais

See also page 176

Paris, La Cité, 1912
Essen, Folkwang Mus.

Signac himself experimented with various media. As well as oil paintings and watercolors he made etchings, lithographs, and many pen-and-ink sketches composed of small, laborious dots. His methods in general were more precise and scientific than Seurat's, his painting richer in color and more luminous. He influenced Henri Matisse and André Derain, thus playing a decisive role in the evolution of Fauvism. When he died in Paris in 1935, however, the style to which he dedicated himself had long ceased to be revolutionary.

The Square at Argenteuil (detail) 1872
Paris, Mus. de l'Impressionnisme

ALFRED SISLEY   1839-1899

A minor figure, but one of the most consistent in the Impressionist movement

Alfred Sisley was born in Paris of English parents, and apart from a few visits to London, where he was sent to learn English, he spent his life in France. His father intended him to take up a career in commerce, but in 1862 he enrolled in the Paris École des Beaux-Arts. In Charles Gleyre's studio there he met Monet, Renoir, and Bazille. Linked by a common dissatisfaction with official arts, typified by the academicism of their teacher Gleyre, the four students formed a clique apart from the others. They spent several summers together in the Forest of Fontainebleau in order to paint in the open.

The work of an outdoor painter of the previous generation, Corot, made a deep impression on Sisley. In the summer of 1867 he worked for the first time at another of Monet's favorite haunts, Honfleur. In 1869, with Monet and Camille Pissarro, he began to give particular attention to the rendering of winter landscape. Whenever he was in Paris, he would spend long evenings at the Café Guerbois, debating with the others the theory of open-air painting. His own subject-matter

The Île Saint-Denis, 1873
Paris, Mus. de l'Impressionnisme

The Orchard, 1881
Rotterdam, Boymans-van Beuningen

scarcely varied. It consisted mainly of the countryside around Paris, and his finest works are perhaps the flood scenes painted at Bougival in 1876.

He had exhibited since 1863, when he showed at the Salon des Refusés. Three years later two canvases were accepted for the Salon proper.

After the Franco-Prussian war, Sisley began to paint in Argenteuil and other districts on the outskirts of Paris. He worked alone, clinging more and more to his sense of isolation. Despite the evidence of his timid, retiring nature, his style gained a new assurance.

He exhibited in the first Impressionist group show, 1874, and most subsequent ones; he suffered financially with the other members in the two disastrous auction sales that they held at the Hôtel Drouot.

Although he started life in comfortable circumstances, the war and the Commune which followed it had deprived his father of his capital and Sisley himself suffered a poverty that was never alleviated, despite the efforts of Charles Durand-Ruel and another dealer, Charpentier, to help him.

In later years his work was shown in the United States, London, and Paris, but it failed to pick up good prices. After a one-man exhibition organized for him in Paris by Durand-Ruel, he moved even farther out of town, to Saint-Mammes. In 1899, sending for Monet, who hurried to his side, he died in Moret-sur-Loing of cancer of the throat. Within a year his canvases were fetching high prices.

Sisley

Landscape
Rennes, Mus. de Rennes

HIS WORKS INCLUDE

View of the Canal Saint-Martin, 1870
Paris, Mus. de l'Impressionnisme

Snow at Louveciennes, about 1874
London, Courtauld Inst. Gall.

The Marly Pond, 1875
London, Tate

Floods at Moret, about 1879
New York, Brooklyn Mus.

La Croix-Blanche at Saint-Mammes 1884
Boston, Mass., Mus. of Fine Arts

See also page 148

Seated Nude, The Black Hat, 1898
London, Tate

An English Impressionist painter and teacher

Philip Wilson Steer was born on December 28, 1860, at Birkenhead, England. His ancestors were Devon yeoman farmers and shipbuilders. His father, an art teacher, had moved north in order to take up a post there. When Steer was four the family moved to Ross-on-Wye, Herefordshire, where his father died seven years later. As a child he had plenty of opportunity and encouragement to experiment with drawing and painting. He came across a book containing engravings of the old masters shown in the Manchester Exhibition of 1857. His careful scrutiny of these left him with a great admiration for Turner. He went to Hereford Cathedral School and Gloucester Art School.

In 1882 Steer went to Paris, where he entered the Académie Julian and a year later the École des Beaux-Arts. He had to leave the latter when it was made compulsory to pass an examination in French. So he returned to England, having seen little of contemporary French art apart from the 1883 Édouard Manet memorial exhibition. Back in London he took a studio, working and teaching all the winter and spending the summers by the sea.

In 1886, aged 26, Steer was a founder member of the New English Art Club, which brought him into contact with Whistler. The club stood firm against

Mrs. Raynes, 1922
London, Tate

The Bridge, Étaples, 1887
London, Tate

William Morris's condemnation of modern painting and made it its aim to use everyday things for subject-matter. Steer was greatly concerned with the visible world and made innumerable landscape studies. He loved the sea, and one of his favorite themes was young girls on the shore. The blurred, misty quality of his *On the Pier-head*, 1887, aroused public antagonism.

About 1888 his mature style established itself and for about five years he was the most advanced painter in England. The dominant influences on him of Whistler and Manet gave way to a clear awareness of Impressionism. An exhibition of Impressionist paintings held in the early 1880's at Dowdeswells was his first introduction to Monet and Renoir, and in 1889 there was another Impressionist exhibition, in Goupil's London gallery.

After some years, however, Steer's style changed. He began to work up his pictures at home rather than paint entirely direct from nature. His color became heavier, his forms more substantial. The painters who then inspired him were Constable, Gainsborough, Rubens, and Tintoretto. For 31 years, from 1899 to 1930, he taught at the Slade School of Art, London, finding gentle phrases for his criticism and giving more attention to his students' sense of color than to anything else. He was influenced by his fellow teacher Henry Tonks and particularly by Turner.

Steer held many exhibitions. His first one-man show was in 1894 and he had a retrospective exhibition at the Tate Gallery in 1929. But although his work was usually pleasing, he failed to live up to his earlier promise. By 1940 his eyesight, which had been deteriorating for some time, was almost totally gone. He died on March 21, 1942.

D. S. McColl Life, Work, and Setting of Philip Wilson Steer London, 1945

HIS WORKS INCLUDE

Southwold, about 1887
London, Tate
Figures on the Beach, Walberswick
1888
London, Tate
Rose Pettigrew, 1891
Glasgow, Art Gall.
The Blue Girl, 1909
Dublin, Gall. of Mod. Art
The Deserted Quarry, Ironbridge
1910
Manchester, England, City Art Gall.
Dover Harbor in War, 1918
London, Imperial War Mus.

See also page 192

Chepstow Castle, 1905
London, Tate

The Music Room, 1906
London, Tate

Two Workers
Amsterdam, Rijksmus.

JAN TOOROP 1858-1928

A Dutch painter and designer within the evolution of Art Nouveau

Jan Toorop was born on December 20, 1858, in Purworedjo in Java, a background that was to mark his work. His father was part Javanese, his mother of British extraction. In 1869 he went to Holland, where he became a pupil of Tetar van Elven. From 1880 to 1885 he studied successively at the Academies of Amsterdam and Brussels and was influenced by the works of Jules Bastien-Lepage, Édouard Manet, and James Ensor. In 1885 he visited England with the Symbolist poet Émile Verhaeren and there discovered the work of William Blake and the Pre-Raphaelites. The following year he married a girl of English-Scottish birth, and lived partly in London, partly in Brussels, until he settled in The Hague in 1889.

In sympathy with every new trend in art, Toorop experimented first with Impressionism. Then the work of Vincent van Gogh and Paul Signac drew him toward Neo-Impressionism. Contact with Ensor and the Brussels Société des XX, with Verhaeren and the writer Maurice Maeterlinck, brought him into the Symbolist orbit. By 1891 Toorop was himself a fully matured Symbolist and certainly the most significant artist in the movement in Holland, an allegiance that was finally confirmed in 1905 by his conversion to Roman Catholicism. In 1892 he produced a series of symbolical drawings with a linear, rhythmic emphasis. These include *O Grave, Where is Thy Victory?*. His drawings of 1893 are typical of Art Nouveau. That year and the next the newly founded English art periodical "The

The Scheldt at Veer (detail) 1907
Utrecht, Centraal Mus.

Pablo Casals (detail) 1904
Rotterdam, Boymans-van Beuningen

Studio" illustrated some of his work, which was in many ways similar to that of another of its contributors, Aubrey Beardsley. Toorop's drawing *The Three Brides*, 1893, is a case in point. In 1893 he exhibited in Munich and in 1894 with Les XX.

His art reflected not only its English sources—William Morris, John Ruskin, late Pre-Raphaelitism—but also the interest in Eastern and exotic art current in Holland from the mid-1880's, when imitation batik printing had become popular. In addition to his paintings, drawings, and graphic work, Toorop made furniture designs, rather in the style of the Art Nouveau decorator Henri van de Velde. He died in The Hague on March 3, 1928.

HIS WORKS INCLUDE

After the Strike, 1887
Otterlo, Holland, Kröller-Müller
"O Grave, Where is Thy Victory?"
1892
Amsterdam, Rijksmus., et al.
The Three Brides, 1893
Otterlo, Holland, Kröller-Müller
The Song of Angels, 1895
Otterlo, Holland, Kröller-Müller
Delftsche Slaolie, 1895
Amsterdam, Stedelijk Mus.
The Sea, 1899
Otterlo, Holland, Kröller-Müller
The Canal near Middelburg, 1907
The Hague, Gemeentemus.

See also page 235

HENRI DE TOULOUSE-LAUTREC   1864-1901

A superb draftsman who revolutionized lithography

Henri de Toulouse-Lautrec was born at Albi in November, 1864. His father was Count Alphonse de Toulouse-Lautrec, his mother her husband's first cousin. In 1872 the family moved to Paris and stayed for some years. Lautrec went to school at the Lycée Condorcet, where he met and made a great friend of Maurice Joyant. The family returned to Albi in 1878, and there Lautrec broke his left leg; next year he had another accident while riding. An inherited disease prevented the bones from healing and Lautrec remained a cripple for the rest of his life. He finished his studies at home, passing the first part of his *baccalauréat* in 1881, and took drawing lessons from an animal painter, René Princeteau. He had a natural facility in drawing and a feeling for paint. From the age of 15 until he was 18 he spent his time between Albi, Paris, and Nice, and made many drawings of horses galloping.

In March, 1882, he decided to study painting seriously and enrolled with Léon Bonnat in Paris. On the retirement of Bonnat he went to Fernand Cormon's studio, where he stayed until 1886. At this time his style tended toward the academic. When Émile Bernard, an enthusiast for Cézanne, entered Cormon's studio in 1885, Lautrec painted his portrait, but required 33 sittings. He himself was an admirer of the work of Pierre Puvis de Chavannes, though he painted a parody of Puvis's *The Sacred Grove Dear to the Arts and the Muses*.

The Realist painter Jules Bastien-Lepage, and probably Édouard Manet and Berthe Morisot influenced him; he also admired Jean Louis Forain's work and through it learned to appreciate Edgar Degas. In 1884 he moved into a studio in Montmartre, where he lived for the next 13 years. At one time Suzanne Valadon, the mother of Maurice Utrillo, was his neighbor. Vincent van Gogh met Lautrec late in 1886, and they saw one another fairly often, first at Cormon's, then in Lautrec's studio. They had little in common, but Lautrec to some extent influenced

HENRI DE
TOULOUSE-LAUTREC (photo)

Portrait of Monsier Fourcade, 1889
São Paulo, Mus. and Art Gall.

van Gogh, and also painted a portrait of him. They exhibited together at the cabaret Le Tabourin in 1887. The strongest influence on Lautrec proved to be Japanese prints and Degas, of whose style and spirit he provided in many respects an extension.

His mature style began its evolution in 1885. He became an *habitué* of the Montmartre café life and made it his main subject. When Aristide Bruant opened his cabaret, Le Mirliton, he went there frequently and they became friends. The following year there was an exhibition of his paintings in Le Mirliton and later he designed a poster for Bruant. He also spent many hours in the Élysée-Montmartre making numerous sketches; the Cirque Fernando was also a frequent distraction and his *Au Cirque Fernando* was painted from sketches made there.

In 1888 he was commisioned to illustrate a magazine, and exhibited on the first of several occasions with Les XX in Brussels. The next year, the year in which his childhood friend Maurice Joyant reappeared in his life, a Belgian painter who insulted van Gogh's work found himself challenged to a duel by Lautrec, backed up in the dispute by Paul Signac.

Au Moulin Rouge, La Dance, 1890
Philadelphia, Pa., coll. Henry P. McIlhenny

Jane Avril Dancing, 1892
Paris, Mus. de l'Impressionnisme

That year, 1889, Lautrec also began to exhibit regularly at the Salon des Indépendants. His paintings there included the *Au Bal du Moulin de la Galette*. And when the Moulin Rouge was opened he also used this dancing place and its artists many times in paintings and lithographs: Jane Avril, for example, appeared on several of his posters, and in 1891 he designed a poster for the Moulin Rouge, with the can-can dancers La Goulue and Valentin-le-Désossé. At the Eldorado the singer Yvette Guilbert made her debut; she too was often sketched by Lautrec. However sordid the life around him, he always used it in paintings remarkable for their objectivity and their lack of any comment. When his cousin Tapié de Celeyran came to Paris in 1891 and worked as an intern in a hospital, he seized the chance of watching and painting the operations. Meanwhile Joyant replaced Theo van Gogh at the Boussod and Valadon galleries, and in 1893 Lautrec exhibited there. About this time he made several trips to Holland, Spain, and Portugal, and to London, where he knew Oscar Wilde and Aubrey Beardsley.

His style grew flat and bold, the paint liquid; and he spread himself in the compositional devices and curvilinear shapes which led eventually to Art

The Modiste, 1900
Albi, France, Mus.

The Tête-à-tête Supper, 1899
London, Courtauld Inst. Gall.

Cha-U-Kao, The Female Clown, 1895
Paris, Mus. de l'Impressionnisme

Nouveau. He became more and more interested in depicting movement, often managing to give his figures a feeling of extension into time. Meanwhile his work became increasingly economical, the color more restricted. With greater and greater energy he experimented with graphic art, continually exploring new lithographic techniques. He made no distinction between "fine" and commercial art. There were theater programs and menu cards, besides the various posters. In fact his graphic art had developed considerably, and by 1898 he was producing a large quantity of designs mainly of Montmartre life—brothels, cabarets, women at their toilet.

His own life had been full of various excesses, and in February of the following year he was taken to a sanatorium at Neuilly. There he made from memory a series of circus drawings. In May he left the sanatorium and began to work again, but his health was continually poor. He went home to visit his mother at Malromé and died there on September 9, 1901.

G. Mack   Toulouse-Lautrec   New York, 1938
D. Cooper   Lautrec   London, 1955
H. P. Landolt   Henri de Toulouse-Lautrec   New York, 1955

Hautrec

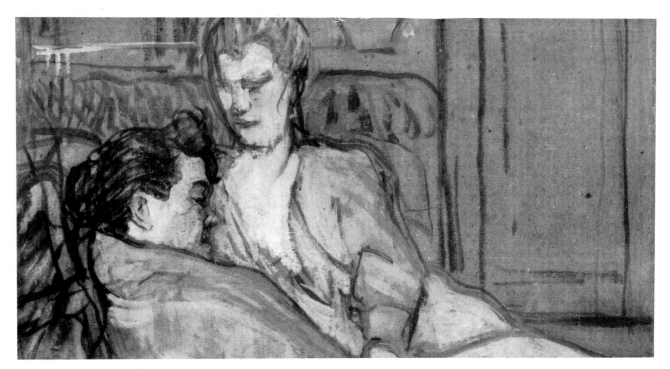

The Two Friends (detail) 1894
London, Tate

ÉDOUARD VUILLARD 1868-1940

A "Nabi" who later turned to domestic subjects in an Impressionist manner

Édouard Vuillard was born on November 11, 1868, at Cuisseaux in the Saône-et-Loire department of France. When he was nine his family moved to Paris. His father, a retired military officer, died in 1883. His mother, who came of a family of textile designers, went into the dressmaking trade in order to support her children. Such an environment must have nurtured Vuillard's sensuous awareness of patterns and textures. He lived with his mother until her death in 1928.

Vuillard was educated, like Toulouse-Lautrec, at the Lycée Condorcet in Paris, where he met Ker Xavier Roussel, who married his sister, and Maurice Denis. In 1886 Vuillard went on, with Roussel, to study painting at the Paris École des Beaux-Arts under the academic Jean Léon Gérôme. Two years later he was working with Denis, his lifelong friend Pierre Bonnard, and Paul Sérusier at the Académie Julian.

That year, 1888, Sérusier met Gauguin at Pont-Aven in Brittany and later brought back with him a painting, *The Talisman*, of an entirely new type, the

PIERRE BONNARD
Portrait of Édouard Vuillard,
about 1891
London, Lefevre Gall.

The Chat, about 1892
Edinburgh, N. G. of Scotland

Under the Trees, 1894
Cleveland, Ohio, Mus. of Art, Hanna Fund

result of taking literally Gauguin's advice to paint in unmodulated, unshaded, unadulterated colors. Out of Sérusier's enthusiasm a group called the Nabis, after the Hebrew for "Prophets," was formed. Vuillard, Bonnard, Denis, and Roussel all became members.

The Nabi painters rejected naturalism and, by implication, Impressionism, in favor of pure design and color. Art, they felt, was more important than nature. Their subject-matter and theories were allied to those of the Symbolist writers and poets, such as Stéphane Mallarmé, an acquaintance of Vuillard. The group held

A Mother and Baby, about 1899
Glasgow, Art Gall.

ritual dinners and discussions and referred to Sérusier's studio as "The Temple."

In 1891 Vuillard shared a studio with Bonnard and Denis. In the same year he contributed to the exhibition of Impressionist and Symbolist painters with which the art dealer Le Barc de Boutteville opened a new Paris gallery. Vuillard focused his attention on the decorative element of painting, producing warm, colorful surfaces that did not attempt to give the illusion of depth. The freedom with which he treated natural forms in the service of design was even greater than that of the Japanese prints that inspired him. But he also bore in mind the firm basic structure of these woodcuts, planning his own work in planes, verticals, and horizontals, within which the patterns could flow.

In 1891 the Symbolist "La Revue Blanche" published lithographs by Vuillard, and he went on to design several covers and posters for it; he also designed murals for one of its founders. He did costumes and sets for the Théâtre de l'Oeuvre in 1893, sets and panels that included a scene from Molière's "Le Malade Imaginaire" for the Comédie des Champs-Élysées in 1913, decorations for the Palais de

In the Park, about 1900
Paris, Mus. d'Art Moderne

E Vuillard

Chaillot in 1937 and, in 1939, decorations, one representing *Peace*, for the League of Nations in Geneva.

With Bonnard, Vuillard visited Hamburg in 1905, England and Holland in 1913. In 1908 he taught at an academy founded by the widow of Paul Ranson, also a Nabi. After 1900, however, their corporate momentum gone, the Nabis disintegrated. Vuillard himself grew closer to the Impressionism that the Nabis had rejected. His work, less colorful and less inventive, consisted now of domestic scenes. He and Bonnard, whose style underwent a similar change, became known as Intimistes.

For some years Vuillard was almost completely out of the public eye, but in 1936 he showed with other former Nabis, and in 1938 a Vuillard retrospective exhibition in Paris revived interest in him. The part played by his pre-Intimiste style in the emergence of Art Nouveau was important. He died on June 21, 1940, at La Baule on the Brittany coast.

A. C. Ritchie Vuillard New York, 1954

Girl in an Interior (detail) 1910-15
London, Tate

The Laden Table, about 1908
London, Tate

JAMES ABBOTT McNEILL WHISTLER 1834-1903

An American-born painter who led the reaction against naturalism in English art

James Abbott McNeill Whistler was born in Lowell, Massachusetts, the son of an army officer who had become an engineer and traveled widely in the exercise of his profession. From 1842 to 1849 the family lived mostly in St. Petersburg, Russia. Whistler took his first art lessons at the Academy of Fine Arts there.

On the death of his father in 1849, Whistler went back to America. In 1851 he enrolled at West Point Military Academy, but three years later was dismissed. He worked for some time in Washington for the United States Coast and Geodetic Service, in which he received a useful training in etching. In 1855 he left America, never to return, and went to Paris to study art. He joined Charles Gleyre's studio and threw himself enthusiastically into the student life of the Left Bank. He made friends with Henri Fantin-Latour and met Gustave Courbet, who offered him occasional advice and influenced his early style. In 1859 Whistler painted *At the Piano*, a composition revolutionary in its informality, and owing something to Manet, Degas, and Japanese prints, as well as to Courbet. When the Salon jury rejected it he exhibited it privately.

Later that year he spent some months near Wapping Pier in London, making a series of etchings of the river Thames. The impression Goya had made on him at

Self-portrait, about 1858
Washington, D. C., Freer Gall. of Art

The Coast of Brittany, 1861
Hartford, Conn., Wadsworth Atheneum

Venice (detail)
London, B. M., et al.

121

an exhibition in Manchester of Spanish painting, which he saw in 1857, is evident, as it is in most of his graphic work.

In England, too, Whistler met Joanna Hefferman, an Irish girl who became his model and his mistress. In 1861 he took her to France. Courbet painted Jo, with her marvellous red hair, in *La Belle Irlandaise*. Whistler painted her all in white against a white backgound in *The White Girl*, exhibited in 1863 at the Salon des Refusés. The female type in Whistler's pictures was possibly borrowed from Dante Gabriel Rossetti, but there was none of Rossetti's intense tragic quality. In fact this painting was a demonstration of Whistler's conviction that subject-matter was unimportant.

After a journey to Spain in 1862, Whistler settled permanently in London, eventually taking a house in Cheyne Walk on the Thames at Chelsea. He helped to introduce into England a taste for Japanese objects, especially prints, materials, and blue porcelain. The Oriental overtones are obvious in his painting *Princess of the Land of Porcelain*, 1864. They were later assimilated and appeared in his work only indirectly.

The late 1860's and the 1870's were Whistler's most productive period. From it date his atmospheric landscape paintings of the Thames at night, to which he gave the musical title *Nocturnes*. Also painted at this time were the great series of portraits that include those of *The Artist's Mother* and *Thomas Carlyle*, further entitled, *Arrangement in Gray and Black No. 1* and *No. 2* respectively, and the delicate *Portrait*

The Lange Lijzen of the Six Marks
Philadelphia, Pa., John G. Johnson Coll.

Valparaiso: Crepuscule in Flesh Color and Green, 1866
London, Tate

of Miss Cecily Alexander, Harmony in Gray and Green, in the background of which is the butterfly motif that Whistler adopted as a signature.

This heyday of his work and social life was shattered by the outcome of a libel suit that he brought against John Ruskin, who in 1877 had violently attacked the paintings Whistler was showing at the Grosvenor Gallery. Ruskin had "never expected to hear a coxcomb ask 200 guineas for flinging a pot of paint in the public's face." Whistler won his case, but he received only one farthing damages, and each party was ordered to pay his own costs. While public subscription covered Ruskin's costs, Whistler went bankrupt. Neither the jury nor the public liked

Portrait of Thomas Carlyle, about 1872
Glasgow, Art Gall.

The Little White Girl: Symphony in
White No. II, 1864   *London, Tate*

the *Nocturnes*, whose impressionistic and vaporous forms had been the cause of the trouble. Questioned about the length of time taken to paint them, Whistler replied that he asked his price not for two days' work but "for the knowledge of a lifetime."

In Venice from 1879 to 1880, he produced a series of pastels and etchings. The prints, which have the shimmering light of the city for their subject, are an original contribution to graphic art. When Whistler returned to London he was gradually able to sell his work and remake his life. But the bitterness remained and the less pleasant, caustic side of his nature emerged. He had always been vain and opinionated, considering the artist to be above normal criticism. Now his doctrine "art for art's sake" became an obsession. The style of his wit resembled that of his much younger acquaintance Oscar Wilde, though in a more barbed and personal vein. He gathered around him an adulatory group of people; Walter Sickert was a devoted follower for a while. The Society of British Artists made Whistler, for a short

St. Mark's, Venice, about 1880
Cardiff, Nat. Mus. of Wales

time, its president. In 1885 he gave his "Ten o'Clock Lecture" in St. James's Hall, one of the events that mark the 19th-century artistic reaction against naturalism and Impressionism. He published this in 1890 in "The Gentle Art of Making Enemies," the story of his London life, in which the typography, wide margins, and asymmetrical arrangement of the title page, not to mention the contents, were revolutionary. Held in high regard by Philip Wilson Steer, Aubrey Beardsley, and John Singer Sargent as well as by Sickert, Whistler had a great influence on art in Britain, above all in opening British eyes to developments on the other side of the English Channel.

Whistler painted comparatively little in the last 20 years of his life. In 1888 he married Mrs. Godwin, a friend he had long admired. For some years they lived in Paris. The *Portrait of the Artist's Mother* was bought for the French nation in 1891. Whistler was made an officer of the Legion of Honor, and his "Ten o'Clock Lecture" was translated into French. Two years after his wife's death in 1896, he opened the short-lived Académie Whistler in Paris. By 1902, a sick man, he began to destroy the drawings and paintings he thought unsatisfactory. He died in London in 1903.

E. R. and J. Pennell   The Life of Whistler   London, 1908
J. Laver   Whistler   London, revised 1951
H. Gregory   The World of James McNeill Whistler   London, 1961
D. Sutton   Nocturne: The Art of James McNeill Whistler   London, 1963

HIS WORKS INCLUDE

The White Girl, 1862
Washington, D. C., N. G.
The Little White Girl:
Symphony in White No. II, 1864
London, Tate
Nocturne: Blue and Silver-
Cremorne Lights, about 1870
London, Tate
Portrait of the Artist's Mother, 1872
Paris, Mus. de l'Impressionnisme
Portrait of Thomas Carlyle,
about 1872
Glasgow, Art Gall.

See also pages 188, 189

JENS FERDINAND WILLUMSEN   1863-1958

A successful Danish Symbolist and Expressionist painter

Jens Ferdinand Willumsen was born in Copenhagen in 1863. Between the ages of 18 and 22 he studied at the Copenhagen Academy. His accomplished naturalistic paintings were already attracting notice when he saw an exhibition of contemporary French art and left Denmark, in 1888, for Paris and Spain.

In Brittany in 1890 he met Paul Gauguin, who taught him the various techniques of preparing a canvas, mixing colors, carving wood panels, and decorating them in polychrome. He also met members of Gauguin's Symbolist following, including Paul Sérusier, through whom the Nabis group came about. Under these influences and that of Odilon Redon, to whom he was introduced the same year, Willumsen's art entered its second phase. His imagination, fired by new and strange ideas of the evolution of nature, produced strongly decorative paintings, and shallow wood reliefs ornamented with colors and applied metals.

In 1891 he exhibited in Paris at the Salon des Indépendants and with the Nabis at the Impressionist and Symbolist show at Le Barc de Boutteville's gallery. According to one of the Nabis, Maurice Denis, the novelty of Willumsen's work raised a stir in Paris comparable to that caused by Gauguin's Café Volpini exhibition of 1889.

Over the next ten years Willumsen devoted much time to experimenting not

After the Tempest (detail) 1905
Oslo, Nasjonalgall.

FW

only with wood carving but also with sculpture and even architecture. Between 1897 and 1913 he designed the independent art exhibitions building in Copenhagen. At the turn of the century he painted a series of studies in the Jura mountains and in the Alps near Lake Geneva. *The Woman Climber*, 1902, was his tribute to his wife, who accompanied him on these mountaineering expeditions.

Meanwhile he did not neglect his more decorative painting. A commission for three allegorical murals depicting three stages in the life of mother and daughter occupied him a great deal in Paris between 1903 and 1905. His big *Sun and Youth* was painted between 1902 and 1910. Numerous large, broadly designed compositions with over life-size figures followed.

From about 1913 Willumsen developed a new, brilliant range of colors, which his visits to Tunis and Spain in 1914 and 1915 reinforced. This brought him to his third and final phase, a type of Expressionism similar in many ways to that of his Scandinavian contemporary Edvard Munch.

In 1923 the Danish government placed a commission for *The Great Relief*, on which Willumsen had already worked for almost 20 years. Finally placed in the Statens Museum, Copenhagen, in 1928, it consists of many different sorts of colored marble and gilded bronze and a complex grouping of symbolic figures.

Children on the Beach, 1910
Gothenburg, Sweden, Konstmus.

GUSTAVE COURBET The Painter's Studio (detail) 1855 *oil on canvas 141¼ × 234¾ in.*
Paris, Louvre

GUSTAVE COURBET The Bride's Toilet, 1865-70 *oil on canvas* *74×99 in.*
Northampton, Mass., Smith College

GUSTAVE COURBET Stormy Sea, 1870   *oil on canvas   46×63 in.*
Paris, Louvre

ÉDOUARD MANET Le Déjeuner sur l'Herbe, 1863 *oil on canvas* 84¼ × 106¼ *in.*
Paris, Musée de l'Impressionnisme

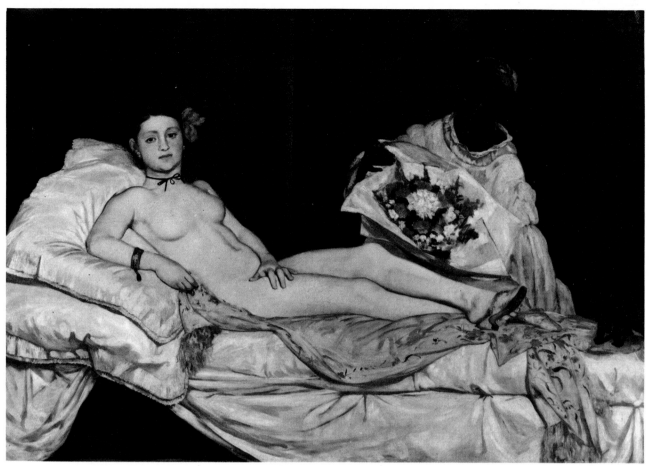

ÉDOUARD MANET Olympia, 1863 *oil on canvas* $51\frac{1}{4} \times 72\frac{3}{4}$ *in.*
Paris, Musée de l'Impressionnisme

ÉDOUARD MANET Le Déjeuner, 1868 *oil on canvas* *44×59¾ in.*
Munich, Neue Pinakothek

ÉDOUARD MANET The Bar at the Folies Bergères, 1882 *oil on canvas* *37½ × 51 in.*
London, Courtauld Institute Galleries

EDGAR DEGAS The Bellelli Family, 1859 *oil on canvas* $78\frac{3}{4} \times 99\frac{5}{8}$ *in.*
Paris, Musée de l'Impressionnisme

EDGAR DEGAS The Dancing Class, 1874 *oil on canvas* $33\frac{1}{2} \times 29\frac{1}{2}$ in.
Paris, Musée de l'Impressionnisme

EDGAR DEGAS The Absinthe Drinker, 1876 *oil on canvas* *36¼ × 27 in.*
Paris, Musée de l'Impressionnisme

EDGAR DEGAS   After the Bath: Woman Drying herself, about 1890   *pastel* $40\frac{1}{2} \times 39$ *in.*
London, National Gallery

137

EUGÈNE BOUDIN   The Empress Eugénie at Trouville, 1863   *oil on panel $13\frac{5}{8} \times 22\frac{1}{2}$ in.*
Glasgow, Art Gallery, Burrell Collection

FRÉDÉRIC BAZILLE   The Artist's Family on the Terrace, 1869   *oil on canvas $59\frac{5}{8} \times 91\frac{3}{8}$ in.*
Paris, Musée de l'Impressionnisme

CLAUDE MONET   The Garden of the Princess, Louvre, about 1866
oil on canvas $36\frac{1}{8} \times 24\frac{3}{8}$ in.
Oberlin, Ohio, Oberlin College, Allen Memorial Art Museum

CLAUDE MONET Women in the Garden, 1867 *oil on canvas $100\frac{3}{8} \times 79$ in.*
Paris, Musée de l'Impressionnisme

141

CLAUDE MONET Impression: Sunrise, 1872 *oil on canvas* $18\frac{7}{8} \times 24\frac{3}{4}$ *in.*
Paris, Musée Marmottan

CLAUDE MONET Boat on the Epte, about 1887   *oil on canvas $52\frac{3}{8} \times 57$ in.*
São Paolo, Museum and Art Gallery

CLAUDE MONET The Haystack, 1891   *oil on canvas   25¼ × 36 in.*
Edinburgh, National Gallery of Scotland, collection Sir Alexander Maitland

CLAUDE MONET Water Lilies, Midday, 1918 *oil on canvas* $78\frac{3}{4} \times 83\frac{5}{8}$ *in.*
Zürich, Bührle Collection

CAMILLE PISSARRO Louveciennes Road, 1870 *oil on canvas* *17¾ × 21¼ in.*
Paris, Musée de l'Impressionnisme

CAMILLE PISSARRO   Orchard in Flower, Pontoise, 1877   *oil on canvas* $25\frac{5}{8} \times 32\frac{7}{8}$ *in.*
Paris, Musée de l'Impressionnisme

ALFRED SISLEY Flood at Marly, 1876 *oil on canvas* $23\frac{5}{8} \times 31\frac{7}{8}$ *in.*
Paris, Musée de l'Impressionnisme

PIERRE AUGUSTE RENOIR La Grenouillère, 1868 *oil on canvas* $25\frac{5}{8} \times 36\frac{5}{8}$ *in.*
Winterthur, Switzerland, Oskar Reinhardt Collection

PIERRE AUGUSTE RENOIR Les Parapluies, 1881-86 *oil on canvas* $70\frac{1}{2} \times 44\frac{1}{2}$ *in.*
London, National Gallery

PIERRE AUGUSTE RENOIR   Bather Drying Herself, about 1910   *oil on canvas* $33\frac{1}{8} \times 25\frac{5}{8}$ *in.*
São Paolo, Museum and Art Gallery

PAUL CÉZANNE The House of the Hanged Man at Auvers-sur-Oise, 1873 *oil on canvas* *21⅞ × 26¼ in.*
Paris, Musée de l'Impressionnisme

PAUL CÉZANNE L'Estaque, about 1883   *oil on canvas* $28\frac{3}{4} \times 35\frac{7}{8}$ in.
São Paolo, Museum and Art Gallery

PAUL CÉZANNE   Still-life with a Basket, about 1890   *oil on canvas* $25\frac{5}{8} \times 31\frac{7}{8}$ *in.*
Paris, Musée de l'Impressionnisme

PAUL CÉZANNE   The Card Players, about 1890   *oil on canvas* $38\frac{1}{4} \times 51\frac{1}{4}$ *in.*
Paris, Musée de l'Impressionnisme

PAUL CÉZANNE The Bathers, 1898-1905 *oil on canvas* *82 × 99 in.*
Philadelphia, Pa., Museum of Art, collection W. P. Wilstach

PAUL CÉZANNE   Mont Sainte-Victoire, about 1906   *oil on canvas   29¼ × 37 in.*
Philadelphia, Pa., Museum of Art, collection George W. Elkins

GUSTAVE MOREAU Thracian Girl with the Head of Orpheus, 1865
oil on canvas   61 × 39⅜ in.
Paris, Musée de l'Impressionnisme

PIERRE PUVIS DE CHAVANNES The Poor Fisherman, 1881   *oil on canvas   61 × 75½ in.*
Paris, Musée de l'Impressionnisme

ODILON REDON Cyclops, 1895-1900 *oil on panel* *25¼ × 20 in.*
Otterlo, Holland, Rijksmuseum Kröller-Müller

ODILON REDON Wildflowers in a Vase, after 1912   *oil on canvas* $28\frac{1}{2} \times 21\frac{1}{8}$ *in.*
Paris, Musée de l'Impressionnisme

GEORGES SEURAT   Une Baignade, about 1884   *oil on canvas* $79\frac{5}{8} \times 118\frac{1}{8}$ *in.*
London, National Gallery

GEORGES SEURAT A Sunday Afternoon on the Island of La Grande Jatte, 1885 *oil on canvas* 81 × 120⅜ in.
Chicago, Art Institute, Helen Birch Bartlett Memorial Collection

GEORGES SEURAT   Harbor at Gravelines, 1890   *oil on canvas   29 × 34¾ in.*
Indianapolis, Herron Museum of Art

GEORGES SEURAT The Circus, 1891   *oil on canvas*   *73 × 60 in.*
Paris, Musée de l'Impressionnisme

PAUL GAUGUIN The Vision after the Sermon—Jacob Wrestling with the Angel, 1888 *oil on canvas* *28¼ × 36½ in.*
Edinburgh, National Gallery of Scotland

PAUL GAUGUIN Loss of Virginity, about 1891   *oil on canvas* $35\frac{1}{4} \times 51\frac{1}{4}$ *in.*
New York, collection Walter P. Chrysler

PAUL GAUGUIN Nave, Nave Mahana, 1896   *oil on canvas* $37\frac{3}{8} \times 51\frac{1}{4}$ *in.*
Lyons, Musée des Beaux-Arts

PAUL GAUGUIN Nevermore, 1897 *oil on canvas* *23⅝ × 46 in.*
London, Courtauld Institute Galleries

VINCENT VAN GOGH Study for the Potato Eaters, 1885   *oil on canvas   28¼×36⅝ in.*
Otterlo, Holland, Rijksmuseum Kröller-Müller

VINCENT VAN GOGH Interior of a Restaurant, 1887 *oil on canvas 18 × 22¼ in.*
Otterlo, Holland, Rijksmuseum Kröller-Müller

VINCENT VAN GOGH L'Arlésienne (Madame Ginoux) 1888 *oil on canvas* *36 × 29 in.*
New York, Metropolitan Museum of Art, Samuel A. Lewisohn Bequest

VINCENT VAN GOGH Self-portrait with a Bandaged Ear, 1888 *oil on canvas* $19\frac{3}{4} \times 17\frac{3}{4}$ *in.*
Chicago, collection Mr. and Mrs. Leigh B. Block

VINCENT VAN GOGH Starry Night, 1889   *oil on canvas   29 × 36¼ in.*
New York, Museum of Modern Art, Lillie P. Bliss Bequest

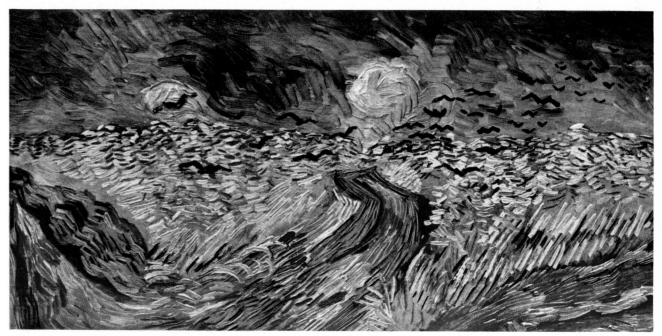

VINCENT VAN GOGH Crows over a Wheat Field, 1890 *oil on canvas 20 × 40¾ in.*
Amsterdam, Stedelijk Museum, V. M. van Gogh Collection

PAUL SIGNAC Le Déjeuner, about 1887 *oil on canvas 35 × 45¼ in.*
Otterlo, Holland, Rijksmuseum Kröller-Müller

HENRI DE TOULOUSE-LAUTREC   Au Cirque Fernando, 1888   *oil on canvas*   *39¼ × 63¼ in.*
Chicago, Art Institute

HENRI DE TOULOUSE-LAUTREC The Moulin Rouge, 1892 *oil on canvas* $48\frac{3}{8} \times 55\frac{1}{4}$ *in.*
Chicago, Art Institute, Helen Birch Bartlett Memorial Collection

HENRI DE TOULOUSE-LAUTREC Study for the Salon in Rue des Moulins, 1893 *oil and chalk on board* $23\frac{5}{8} \times 31\frac{1}{2}$ *in.*
São Paolo, Museum and Art Gallery

PIERRE BONNARD Le Déjeuner, 1899 *oil on canvas 21½ × 27¾ in.*
Zürich, Bührle Collection, Foundation E. G. Bührle

ÉDOUARD VUILLARD The Flowered Robe, 1891 *oil on canvas 15 × 18⅝ in.*
São Paolo, Museum and Art Gallery

HENRI ROUSSEAU War, 1894 *oil on canvas* $44\frac{1}{2} \times 76$ *in.*
Paris, Musée de l'Impressionnisme

HENRI ROUSSEAU Football Players, 1908 *oil on canvas* $39\frac{1}{2} \times 31\frac{5}{8}$ *in.*
New York, Solomon R. Guggenheim Museum Collection

JAKOB MARIS Dordrecht *oil on canvas* *36¼ × 43½ in.*
Glasgow, Art Gallery, Burrell Collection

CARL FREDRIK HILL Landscape, 1877 *oil on canvas* $19\frac{5}{8} \times 23\frac{5}{8}$ *in.*
Stockholm, Nationalmuseum

THOMAS EAKINS Max Schmitt in a Single Scull, 1871 *oil on canvas* $32\frac{1}{4} \times 46\frac{1}{4}$ *in.*
New York, Metropolitan Museum of Art, Alfred N. Punnett Fund and Gift of George D. Pratt

WINSLOW HOMER Long Branch, New Jersey, 1869 *oil on canvas 16 × 21¾ in.*
Boston, Mass., Museum of Fine Arts

JAMES ABBOTT McNEILL WHISTLER   Portrait of the Artist's Mother, 1872   *oil on canvas*   *57 × 62½ in.*
Paris, Musée de l'Impressionnisme

JAMES ABBOTT McNEILL WHISTLER   Nocturne in Black and Gold: The Falling Rocket
about 1874   *oil on panel $23\frac{3}{4} \times 18\frac{3}{8}$ in.*
Detroit, Mich., Institute of Arts

MARY CASSATT The Bath, about 1891   *oil on canvas*   *39¼ × 26 in.*
Chicago, Art Institute

JOHN SINGER SARGENT Portrait of Robert Louis Stevenson, 1885 *oil on canvas 20 × 24 in.*
New York, John Hay Whitney Collection

PHILIP WILSON STEER   The Beach at Walberswick. 1890   *oil on canvas   23¼ × 29¼ in.*
London, Tate Gallery

WALTER RICHARD SICKERT   The Old Bedford Music Hall, about 1895   *oil on canvas   30 × 25⅝ in.*
Liverpool, England, Walker Art Gallery

WILHELM LEIBL The Spinner, 1892 *oil on canvas* $25\frac{1}{4} \times 29\frac{1}{8}$ *in.*
Leipzig, Museum of Fine Arts

MAX LIEBERMANN The Parrot Man, 1902 *oil on canvas 40 × 28¼ in.*
Essen, Gemäldesammlung

DANTE GABRIEL ROSSETTI Lady Lilith *oil on canvas* *37½ × 32 in.*
Wilmington, Del., Society of Fine Arts, Bancroft Collection

SIR EDWARD COLEY BURNE-JONES Love Among the Ruins, 1894 *oil on canvas* *37 × 63 in.*
Wolverhampton, England, Wightwick Manor, National Trust

HANS VON MARÉES St. Hubert, from the Triptych, about 1887   *oil on panel*   *72 × 43¼ in.*
Munich, Neue Pinakothek

ARNOLD BÖCKLIN   The Island of the Dead, 1880   *tempera on canvas*   *43$\frac{3}{4}$×61 in.*
Basel, Öffentliche Kunstsammlung, Gottfried Keller Foundation

ALBERT PINKHAM RYDER Toilers of the Sea *oil on panel 11¼ × 12 in.*
New York, Metropolitan Museum of Art, George A. Hearn Fund

GIOVANNI SEGANTINI Love at the Fount of Life, 1896 *oil on canvas* $28\frac{3}{8} \times 39\frac{3}{8}$ *in.*
Milan, Galleria Civica d'Arte Moderna

JAMES ENSOR The Entry of Christ into Brussels in 1889 (detail) 1888 *oil on canvas* $101\frac{1}{2} \times 169\frac{3}{4}$ *in.*
Antwerp, Musée Royal des Beaux-Arts, lent by Mrs. Louis Franck, London

JENS FERDINAND WILLUMSEN Montagnes Russes, 1890   *oil on canvas* $49\frac{1}{4} \times 58\frac{3}{4}$ *in.*
Oslo, Nasjonalgalleriet

GUSTAV KLIMT The Kiss, 1908 *oil on canvas $70\frac{7}{8} \times 70\frac{7}{8}$ in.*
Vienna, Österreichische Galerie

FERDINAND HODLER Night, 1890 *oil on canvas* $45\frac{5}{8} \times 117\frac{3}{4}$ *in.*
Berne, Kunstmuseum

EDVARD MUNCH The Cry, 1893 *oil and tempera on cardboard* $35\frac{7}{8} \times 28\frac{7}{8}$ *in.*
Oslo, Munch-Museet

EDVARD MUNCH The Dance of Life, about 1900   *oil on canvas* $40\frac{1}{2} \times 75$ *in.*
Oslo, Nasjonalgalleriet

LOVIS CORINTH Self-portrait, 1914 *oil on panel* $28\frac{3}{4} \times 22\frac{5}{8}$ *in.*
Munich, Neue Pinakothek

Drawings

PIERRE PUVIS DE CHAVANNES The Toilet *black chalk*
Paris, Louvre

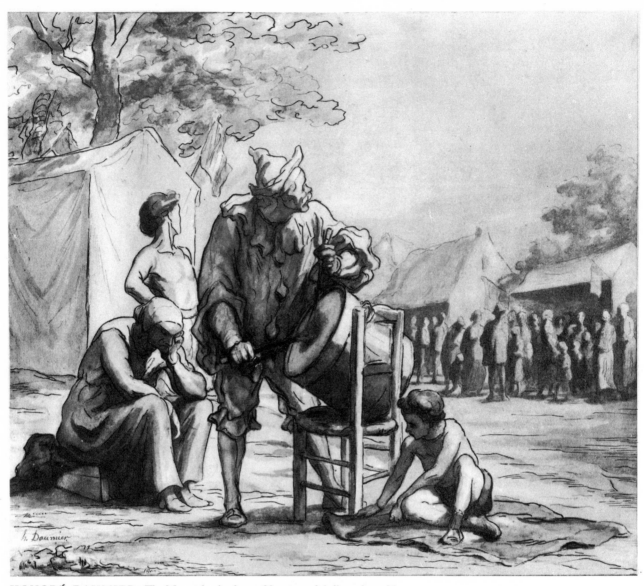

HONORÉ DAUMIER The Mountebank, about 1860 *pen and chalk* $13\frac{1}{4} \times 15\frac{5}{8}$ *in.*
London, Victoria and Albert Museum

JEAN FRANÇOIS MILLET Maternal Vigil, about 1861 *black chalk* *12 × 10¼ in.*
Birmingham, England, City Museum and Art Gallery

JOHAN BARTHOLD JONGKIND Antwerp Harbor, 1868 *etching* 6×9¼ *in.*
London, British Museum, et al.

CAMILLE PISSARRO The Market *etching* $7\frac{7}{8} \times 5\frac{1}{4}$ *in.*
London, British Museum, et al.

ÉDOUARD MANET   Portrait of the Critic Charles Baudelaire, 1862
etching   5⅛ × 3 in.
London, Courtauld Institute Galleries, et al.

EDGAR DEGAS Self-portrait *red chalk* $13\frac{1}{4} \times 9\frac{3}{4}$ *in.*
Providence, R. I., Private Collection

PIERRE AUGUSTE RENOIR   Study for a Portrait of Julie Manet   *black chalk   23⅞ × 18¼ in.*
Paris, Durand-Ruel et Cie

PAUL CÉZANNE   Achille Emperaire   *black chalk* $4\frac{7}{8} \times 3$ *in.*
Basel, Kupferstichkabinett

PAUL CÉZANNE A Peasant, about 1897 *pencil* *15 × 11¾ in.*
Basel, Kupferstichkabinett

EDGAR DEGAS A Woman Bathing *black chalk 14⅛ × 12 in.*
Rotterdam, Boymans-van Beuningen Museum

CLAUDE MONET Rocks at Belle-Île   *black chalk* $9 \times 12\frac{1}{8}$ *in.*
Paris, Durand-Ruel et Cie

VINCENT VAN GOGH View of Saintes-Maries, 1888 *watercolor*
St. Louis, Mo., collection Mr. and Mrs. Joseph Pulitzer

VINCENT VAN GOGH Wild Vegetation, 1890 *ink and watercolor* *18¼ × 24 in.*
Amsterdam, Stedelijk Museum

PAUL GAUGUIN   Portrait of Stéphane Mallarmé (detail) 1891   *etching* $7\frac{1}{4} \times 5\frac{1}{4}$ *in.*
London, British Museum, et al.

223

GEORGES SEURAT At the "Concert Européen," about 1887 *conté crayon* $12\frac{1}{4} \times 9\frac{3}{8}$ *in.*
New York, Museum of Modern Art

GEORGES SEURAT Place de la Concorde, Winter, 1883-84 *conté crayon* $9\frac{1}{8} \times 12\frac{1}{8}$ *in.*
New York, Solomon R. Guggenheim Museum

225

HENRI DE TOULOUSE-LAUTREC The Dancer Chocolat in the Bar d'Achille
watercolor and chalk $30\frac{3}{8} \times 24$ *in.*
Albi, France, Museum

HENRI DE TOULOUSE-LAUTREC In Bed, about 1896 *pencil 11¼ × 18¾ in.*
London, Courtauld Institute Galleries

5653

AUGUSTE RODIN Female Nude *watercolor and chalk* *12¼ × 9⅛ in.*
Paris, Musée Rodin

ODILON REDON Head of Orpheus *charcoal $16\frac{1}{8} \times 13\frac{3}{8}$ in.*
Otterlo, Holland, Rijksmuseum Kröller-Müller

PIERRE BONNARD The Dogs, 1893 *lithograph* $14\frac{1}{4} \times 10\frac{1}{4}$ in.
New York, Museum of Modern Art, et al.

ÉDOUARD VUILLARD Interior with a Screen, 1895 *lithograph*
Private Collection

EDVARD MUNCH Two People (The Lonely Ones) about 1896 *drypoint* $6 \times 8\frac{1}{2}$ *in.*
Oslo, Nasjonalgalleriet, et al.

JAMES ENSOR The Cathedral, 1886 *etching* $9\frac{1}{4} \times 7$ *in.*
London, British Museum, et al.

CARL FREDRIK HILL   A Preacher in an Icy Wilderness   *black chalk*
Malmö, Sweden, Museum

JAN TOOROP "O Grave, Where is Thy Victory?" 1892 *lithograph* $23\frac{5}{8} \times 29\frac{1}{2}$ *in.*
Amsterdam, Rijksmuseum, et al.

AUBREY BEARDSLEY The Mysterious Rose Garden: from
"The Yellow Book," 1894 *india ink with watercolor*
Location of original unknown

AUBREY BEARDSLEY   Messalina and her Companion, 1896
india ink with watercolor $10\frac{3}{4} \times 6\frac{7}{8}$ in.
London, Tate Gallery

DANTE GABRIEL ROSSETTI Elizabeth Siddall Plaiting her Hair *pencil 6¾ × 5 in.*
London, Tate Gallery

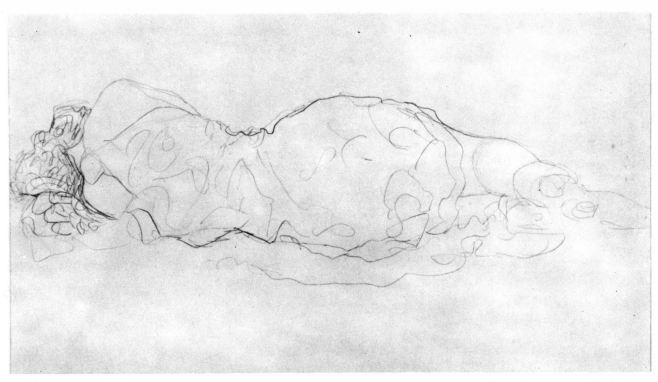

GUSTAV KLIMT Reclining Woman Seen from behind, about 1916 *pencil* 13¾×22⅜ *in.*
Vienna, Albertina

WALTER RICHARD SICKERT La Carolina dell'Aqua, 1903 *black chalk and india ink* *13⅛×9 in.*
Oxford, Ashmolean Museum

Sculpture

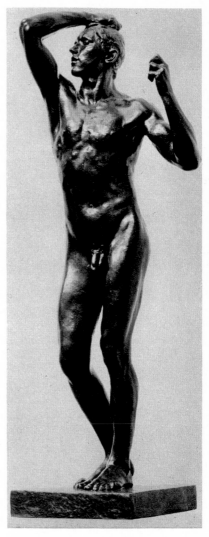

AUGUSTE RODIN   The Age of Bronze, about 1877   *bronze   height 71¼ in.*
London, Tate Gallery, et al.

AUGUSTE RODIN A Man Walking, 1877-1900 *bronze*
Paris, Musée Rodin, et al.

AUGUSTE RODIN Monument to Balzac, about 1897 *plaster height 118 in.*
Paris, Musée Rodin

AUGUSTE RODIN
The Gates of Hell,
1880 - about 1900
bronze height 248 in.
Paris, Musée Rodin, et al.

244

AUGUSTE RODIN Danaïd, 1885   *marble   height 13¾ in.*
Paris, Musée Rodin

JULES DALOU   The French Peasant Woman,
1873
terracotta   height 53¾ *in.*
London, Tate Gallery

246

CONSTANTIN MEUNIER
The Hammerman, 1885
bronze
Copenhagen, Ny Carlsberg Glyptothek

EDGAR DEGAS
Little Dancer Aged 14, about 1881
bronze and fabric height 39 in.
London, Tate Gallery, et al.

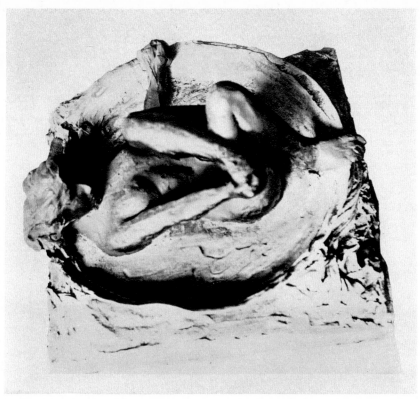

EDGAR DEGAS
The Tub, about 1886 *bronze height 18½ in.*
Paris, Durand-Ruel et Cie, et al.

EDGAR DEGAS
La Grande Arabesque, about 1890
bronze height 19 in.
Providence, R. I., Rhode Island School of Design, et al.

PIERRE AUGUSTE RENOIR The Washerwoman, about 1918 *bronze height 47¾ in.*
London, Tate Gallery, et al.

PAUL GAUGUIN Soyez Amoureuses, Vous Serez Heureuses, 1889 *painted wood relief* $47\frac{1}{8} \times 38\frac{1}{8}$ *in.*
Boston, Mass., Museum of Fine Arts

ARISTIDE MAILLOL Study for Méditerranée, about 1900 *terracotta width 5⅞ in.*
New York. Museum of Modern Art

ANTOINE BOURDELLE Hercules the Archer, 1909   *bronze   height 98 in.*
Rome, Museo Nazionale d'Arte Moderna

253

MEDARDO ROSSO Conversation in the Garden, 1893 *bronze   height* $12\frac{3}{4}$ *in.*
Rome, Museo Nazionale d'Arte Moderna

 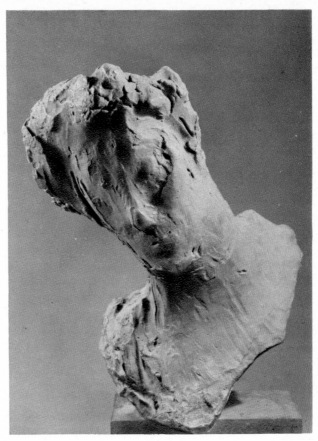

MEDARDO ROSSO Yvette Guilbert, 1894 *wax   height 17⅞ in.*
Rome, Museo Nazionale d'Arte Moderna

MEDARDO ROSSO La Grande Rieuse, 1891 *wax*
Rome, Museo Nazionale d'Arte Moderna

Influences and Developments

Courbet and Realism

The precise origins of the realist movement which emerged in the mid-19th century are difficult to define although it is generally agreed that Gustave Courbet was the first great realist painter of that century. In some respects his work was a continuation of the traditions of the Spanish painters Velázquez and Francisco de Zurbarán, and of the 17th-century Dutch painters, especially Rembrandt.

In expounding his theory on realism Courbet claimed: "The basis of realism is negation of the ideal, a negation toward which my studies have led me for

a

fifteen years and which no artist has dared to affirm categorically until now.....
Romantic art, like that of the Classical school, was art for art's sake. Today, in
accordance with the most recent developments in philosophy, one is obliged to
reason even in art, and never to permit sentiment to overthrow logic. Reason should
be man's ruling principle in everything. My art is the final one because it is the
only one which, so far, has combined all these elements. Through my affirmation
of the negation of the ideal and all that springs from the ideal I have arrived at
the emancipation of the individual and finally at democracy. Realism is essentially the democratic art."

Courbet further maintained that painting was essentially a concrete art concerned with the representation of real existing objects the artist could actually
see and touch. Abstract objects, which were "invisible and non-existent," were
totally inadequate for painting. Art essentially reflected its period, and artists of
one period could not hope to reproduce things of a preceding or future century.

The realist determination to depict everyday life is expressed in *The Painter's
Studio* (b), in which each figure is intended to summarize some aspect of contemporary society. This strong reaction against the accepted conventions for
subject matter is perhaps best illustrated by *The Burial at Ornans* and *The Stone
Breakers* (a), in which the figures of ordinary people are represented in an unpre-
cedented direct and monumental fashion. In these paintings no concessions were
made to sentimentality or elegance. The proletariat and the *petite bourgeoisie* were
henceforth to provide a wide range of pictorial material.

a Gustave Courbet
The Stone Breakers, 1850
*oil on canvas   62¾ × 102 in.
(Destroyed World War II)
Formerly Dresden, Gemäldegalerie*

b Gustave Courbet
The Painter's Studio, 1855
*oil on canvas   141¼ × 234¾ in.
Paris, Louvre*

b

Realism in France

The tradition of using peasant themes as the subject matter of art ran throughout the greater part of the 19th century, and was closely linked with the genre painting that largely derived from the 17th-century Dutch schools. Jean François Millet provided a direct record of the life and work of the peasants amongst whom he had been born and imbued his representations of laborers and the like with his own

a

b

c

d

strong religious feelings. He sought to interpret the Bible in terms of his own daily life and that of the French peasantry. The simplicity and monumentality of his painting are sometimes overlaid with sentimentality. It is the dignity of labor rather than its hardships that is evident in his work, *The Man with a Hoe* (c), although his drawings, such as *Man Carrying a Log* (d), show an uncompromising approach to the subject. Millet had no desire to be considered a radical, and unlike Honoré Daumier he had no political interests.

Daumier also explored the world of the peasant and laborer, but he concentrated on the broader panorama of urban life, which he satirized with a forceful political and social bias. He had none of Millet's sentimentality and an even greater feeling for form and volume, as revealed in *The Washerwoman* (a). His pathos and protest against social injustice replaced the philosophical and religious tones found in Millet. Both painters were able to create an epic and timeless quality from the material of everyday life. Daumier added to this a subjective sense of violence and distortion in the unfinished *Man on a Rope* (b).

a Honoré Daumier
The Washerwoman, 1861
oil on panel $17\frac{3}{4} \times 12\frac{1}{2}$ in.
Paris, Louvre

b Honoré Daumier
Man on a Rope, about 1862
oil on canvas $44\frac{1}{4} \times 29$ in.
Boston, Mass., Museum of Fine Arts

c Jean François Millet
The Man with a Hoe, 1863
oil on canvas $32 \times 39\frac{1}{4}$ in.
Boston, Mass., Museum of Fine Arts,
collection Mrs. H. Potter Russell

d Jean François Millet
Man Carrying a Log, about 1848
black chalk on gray paper $12\frac{1}{8} \times 9\frac{3}{8}$ in.
Cambridge, England,
Fitzwilliam Museum

Realism outside France

Realism in painting became widespread not only in many parts of Europe but also in America. The primary concern for matter-of-fact representation of ordinary daily life was subsequently extended by the introduction of new themes. Certain of these themes, such as the appeal of the sea evident in *Eight Bells* (d) by the American painter Winslow Homer, became part of the realist tradition. The subject tended to be more important than the way in which paint was handled: Homer combined freshness of observation with a sensitive control of light and a complete lack of sentimentality. Painters in Holland and England also illustrate the life of sailors at sea. Another American painter, Thomas Eakins, who was influenced by Velázquez, Édouard Manet, Rembrandt, and José Ribera, painted in a precise factual way many aspects of life in his native Philadelphia. In one of his most ambitious works, *The Agnew Clinic*, 1889 (a), the highly detailed drawing of the figures is counterbalanced by the unifying use of light.

In England the painter Frank Holl spent his life painting scenes from the life

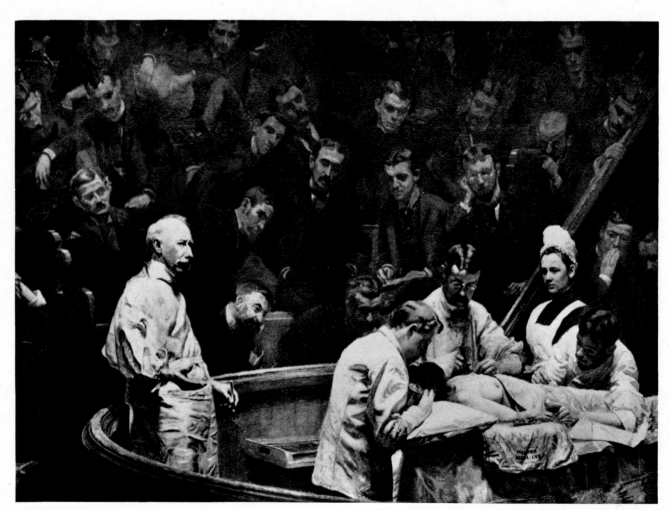

a

around him with great earnestness and a careful attention to detail. Nearly all Holl's paintings are concerned with human poverty and misery, as in *Newgate, Committed for Trial* (b), which van Gogh greatly admired. The painter Wilhelm Leibl in Germany was influenced by Courbet and by the Flemish and German primitives. He carried the representation of the material world to its highest pitch and treated his subjects as still-lifes, as seen in *Three Women in Church* (c).

All these painters were linked in their determination to portray the everyday life around them, and in each case their style of painting was influenced by realist painters of preceding periods.

b

c

d

Thè art of 17th-century Spain and Holland held a spectacular appeal for many painters of the Impressionist generation. Courbet had admired painters such as Velázquez and Zurbarán, but the full impact of the Spanish influence is seen in the

a Henri Fantin-Latour
The Two Sisters, 1859
oil on canvas 39¼ × 52 in.
St. Louis, Mo., City Art Museum

b James Abbott McNeill Whistler
At the Piano, 1859
oil on canvas 26 × 36 in.
Cincinnati, Ohio, Taft Museum,
Louise Taft Semple Bequest

c Édouard Manet
Lola de Valence, 1862
oil on canvas 45½ × 36¼ in.
Paris, Musée de l'Impressionnisme

d Edgar Degas
Young Spartans Exercising
1860 *oil on canvas 43 × 60¾ in.*
London, National Gallery

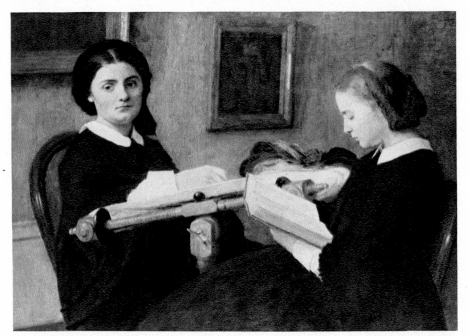

a

b

works of Édouard Manet and James Abbot McNeill Whistler.

During the 1860's a change in style was taking place. The refinement and aristocratic quality of Velázquez found a deep response in the upper middle class painters, who were delighted with his mastery of paint and sense of poise. Manet as a boy saw Louis Philippe's collection of Spanish paintings that was on show to the public in 1838 and remained in the Louvre for ten years. In the 1850's and 1860's there was a vogue for things Spanish: Manet himself made several paintings of a troupe of Spanish dancers that visited Paris. Between 1861 and 1862 he painted *Lola de Valence* (c), which shows both the influence of Spanish subject matter and an interest in the full length portrait derived from a study of Velázquez, many of whose paintings he probably saw during a trip to Vienna in 1853. The direct lighting of the figure, also evident in his *Olympia*, which so disturbed the critics, was a direct result of his admiration for the Spanish school. Similar qualities appear in the work of Whistler, who derived his use of the silvery gray tonality from Velázquez and showed the strong influence of Courbet in his earlier paintings. *At the Piano* (b), demonstrates the new impact of photography, which was to revolutionize the painter's approach to composition. The limited range of colors owes something to Henri Fantin-Latour, Whistler's friend. Edgar Degas was also influenced by photography. His compositions were often unusual and direct in their impact. The *Young Spartans Exercising* (d), painted by Degas in 1860, suggests a classical scene particularly in composition, but instead of imitating the conventional type of Greek figure, he used the urchins from Montmartre as his models.

Fantin-Latour, who was on friendly terms with both Manet and Whistler, turned to the Old Masters for inspiration. He was generally influenced by Dutch painting, and in particular by Vermeer, whose work was then beginning to be appreciated. Fantin's use of light and mass is close to Vermeer, but owes something to the naturalism of portrait photography as well (a).

c

d

a James Abbott McNeill Whistler
The White Girl, 1862
oil on canvas 84½ × 42½ in.
Washington, D.C.,
National Gallery of Art

b Photograph of a wall of a Paris
Salon in the 1860's

The Salon des Refusés

In 1863 the Jury of the Paris Salon was exceptionally severe. It was determined to prevent any errors of the sort that had allowed Manet's *Spanish Guitar Player* to be exhibited two years previously. The Salon authorities rejected over 4000 paintings in their effort to keep out any progressive elements: on no other occasion had so many paintings been refused. Eventually the Emperor Napoleon III intervened and the Salon des Refusés was held in another section of the Palais de l'Industrie so that the public might judge for itself the value of the Jury's decision.

The public and most of the critics greeted the rejected paintings with derision and indignation. Manet's *Le Déjeuner sur l'Herbe* was the focal point of the public scorn, but in the eyes of the younger and more progressive painters it established the artist as the unwilling leader of a revolutionary movement in painting. This paved the way for Impressionism, and had an important influence on Paul Cézanne's style. Among the painters who contributed to the Salon des Refusés were Camille Pissarro, Johan Barthold Jongkind, Cézanne, and Whistler, whose painting, *The White Girl* (a) was another of the sensations of this Salon. The entire painting is light in key and white in color, apart from the model's red hair. It suggested a musical analogy to one of the critics, who called it a "Symphony in White." Whistler was later to take up this idea.

a

b

Japanese Influence in the 1860's

a Utagawa Kuniaki
Portrait of a Wrestler (detail)
color lithograph
London, British Museum, et al.

b Édouard Manet
Portrait of Émile Zola (detail) 1868
oil on canvas $57\frac{1}{4} \times 43\frac{1}{4}$ *in.*
Paris, Musée de l'Impressionnisme

The discovery of Japanese prints was one of the most revolutionary factors in the development of 19th-century art in Europe. There were some early collectors: by about 1850 the engraver Félix Braquemond had assembled a substantial collection in Paris. Some of these prints probably arrived in Europe as wrappings on goods from the Far East. By 1862, however, interest had grown to such an extent that a shop called "La Porte Chinoise" was opened in Paris with prints and pottery amongst its wares. Five years later a large number of Japanese prints were exhibited in the Paris "Exposition Universelle," which certainly made a great impact upon the Parisian artists. Other exhibitions followed and the taste spread rapidly.

A good example of one aspect of Japanese influence can be seen in Manet's *Portrait of Émile Zola* (b), painted in 1868, where the author is depicted in front of a print recognizable as a *Wrestler* by Utagawa Kuniaki. An example of his work is shown in (a). Both Whistler and Claude Monet also made a similar use of Japanese decorations from time to time. Japanese draftsmanship strongly influenced the Impressionists and their associates and was partly responsible for many radical innovations. The typical slicing in half of figures and the close intimate view are seen in the works of Manet, Degas, Monet, and the other Impressionists. The almost obsessive use of the diagonal, the disregard for conventional perspective, and the emphasis on the purely decorative elements of design all stem from the Japanese print.

Degas responded quickly to Japanese prints taking from them those features that interested him. In a great many of his paintings such as *The Absinthe Drinker*, some race course scenes, and paintings of the ballet, he made use of the diagonal motif and the Oriental emphasis on line. Subject matter was to some extent also derived from these prints, but the Impressionists did not follow the Japanese artist all the way to the flattening of form and elimination of shadows. This step was left to a later generation of artists.

a b

Sources of Impressionism

Impressionism was the most important movement in art in the 19th century: it took its name from Monet's painting *Impression: Sunrise* of 1872. As a movement it largely derived from Courbet, the Barbizon painters, and from Eugène Delacroix. *The Hay-Wain* (a) by John Constable, exhibited at the Salon in 1824, greatly impressed Delacroix, particularly with its freshness of vision and use of broken touches of color. It also had a profound effect on all the later French landscape painters. The concern for light, above all, made Constable a precursor of Eugène Boudin, Jongkind, the Barbizon School, and Impressionism.

The practice of painting landscapes in the open air, direct from nature, was developed at the village of Barbizon in the Forest of Fontainebleau. Théodore Rousseau made many free and spontaneous studies of landscape, for example *Montmartre—Stormy Sky* (c), which shows a parallel to Constable in the painter's concern with atmospheric effects. Camille Pissarro was deeply influenced by Jean Baptiste Camille Corot in the early years of his career, and from him derived a concern for structure and composition. Corot's paintings were a clear example of a "natural way of seeing things" and expressed his own dictum that "the first impression by which we are moved" should never be lost. His work is generally characterized by a feeling of luminosity and atmospheric effects, the result of using white mixed with other colors; this use of color values to build up the forms contained in his compositions was extremely important for the growth of Impressionism. His device of a road leading into the depths of a landscape (d) was frequently adopted by most of the Impressionists. Pissarro, for example, while painting in Louveciennes, made particular use of figures in a road.

It is debatable to what extent the Impressionists were influenced by Joseph Mallord William Turner. Both Monet and Pissarro had seen some of his works while visiting London during the Franco-Prussian war and were greatly impressed by his use of color, particularly in rendering the effects of snow and steam (which occurred later in Monet's work) in his painting *Rain, Steam and Speed—The Great Western Railway* (b). While the Impressionists claimed that Turner had not understood the analysis of shadows, they had not seen his late works, such as the paintings of Venice, which were later to influence Monet.

a

b

266

c

d

Impressionist Technique

The Impressionist technique evolved from the search for a means to depict optical truth as exactly as possible. Traditional linear forms of representation were abandoned and the nature of color and light thoroughly explored. The two natural surfaces which presented excellent opportunities for this study were water and snow. The Impressionist approach is clearly seen in Claude Monet's painting of *La Grenouillère* (a and b), where broken touches of color have been used to represent the shimmering light on the water and the contrast of light and shadow. The study of water helped to show the Impressionists that the local color of an object is affected by the surrounding conditions. This knowledge led to the placing of colors side by side to produce an optical mixture, and the intensification of colors by juxtaposing complementaries. The most effective means of achieving the instantaneous and atmospheric impression was to use small dashes and strokes of pure color, freely and quickly applied.

Snowy landscapes were ideal for the observation and analysis of color in shadows. By studying the effects of sunlight on snow the Impressionists realized that no shadows are completely black, that pure colors produced a truer visual image of a dazzling white than white itself. *The Magpie* (c), painted by Monet about 1870, was one of the first experiments in this new approach to light on snow.

a

b

c

Impressionist Subjects

The Impressionists were determined to paint the life around them and to look at their surroundings with fresh eyes. The many and varied aspects of everyday life in Paris with its bustling crowds, streets and suburbs, entertainments and pastimes, now became the scene of exploration and yielded as much variety of subject matter as the surrounding countryside. Of all the Impressionists only Alfred Sisley restricted himself almost entirely to painting landscapes. The "big city," which had been one of the main ideas behind Charles Baudelaire's aesthetic, now became one of the predominant themes of Impressionism.

In the 19th century the choice of everyday and transitory subject matter was an important innovation, and the long battle with academic art was caused by subject matter as well as by style. Pierre Auguste Renoir's great delight in painting pretty girls is evident in *La Loge* (a), of 1874. Camille Pissarro spent most of his time in the country, but in 1897 he took a room in Paris and painted a series of street views; one of these (c) shows a boulevard at night in which the shapes are dissolved in the contrast between the street lights and the shadows. Renoir's *The Luncheon of the Boating Party* (b) represents a summer excursion on the river, which was another aspect of gay Paris life.

a Pierre Auguste Renoir
La Loge, 1874
oil on canvas 31½ × 25 in.
London, Courtauld Institute Galleries

b Pierre Auguste Renoir
The Luncheon of the Boating Party
1881 *oil on canvas 51 × 68 in.*
Washington, D. C.,
Phillips Memorial Gallery

c Camille Pissarro
Paris, the Boulevard Montmartre
at Night, 1897
oil on canvas 15½ × 21 in.
London, National Gallery

a

b

c

Development of Impressionism

By the 1880's there was no longer a consistent approach to art among the Impressionists. Monet's style began to develop away from the others and from his own earlier work. An emotional, non-realistic quality now emerged with the brushwork becoming more violent and calligraphic in style. Impressionism had always been based on the individual sensation and on a sensual reaction to the visual world: this inherent subjectivity became increasingly evident in Monet's paintings. By the 1890's the subject matter was unimportant and no more than a framework for recording the most transitory effects of light. In 1890 Monet began to paint a series of canvases representing an object in the varying conditions of light at different times of the day. Between 1892 and 1893 he painted the Rouen Cathedral series (b), which he afterwards worked up in his studio. These paintings, described by Paul Signac as "marvelously executed walls," show that Monet now considered the perceptual experience of the painter as more important than the natural appearance of the object. The interest in tactile qualities evident in the Cathedral series can also be seen in the *Nymphéas* (or water lily) paintings (a). After 1900 Monet spent most of his time painting in his garden in Giverny. There he had become absorbed in the study of the plants on the water, producing a sense of elemental fusion of water, sky, and flowers. The feeling of involvement in the picture now became a total obsession and culminated in the series of enormous panoramic pictures in the Orangerie, Paris.

Paul Cézanne did not at any time feel that the momentary effects of Impression-

a

b

ism were sufficient for a painting. Consequently he moved steadily away from an Impressionist style, always searching for the underlying, unchanging form of things. In his late work, color, as with Monet, became the sole means of expressing all the separate elements that form a painting and achieved an almost abstract quality. He also realized that the changing reaction of the painter to his subject was all important in the creation of a painting. He was primarily interested in form, color, planes, and light, as in *The Lake of Annecy* (c), where the structure and solidity of each object was equally felt. From Cézanne's attitude to form and color the radical movements of the early 20th century developed.

c

Impressionism outside France

Toward the end of the 19th century the influence of Impressionism was fairly widespread not only in Europe but among the American painters who had visited Paris. The contact with Impressionism resulted in a freer handling of paint and an interest in contemporary subject matter rather than in a strict application of its color theories.

In England Walter Richard Sickert looked to Impressionism for inspiration and revolutionized the approach to art, thus bringing it into line with Continental developments. Sickert was particularly influenced by Edgar Degas, whom he had met in 1883, and many of Degas' ideas, such as the urban subject matter, theater scenes, and a feeling for unorthodox composition, found expression in his work. His

a

b

c

later paintings became brighter in color when he came under the influence of Pissarro and some younger English painters.

Another English painter, Wilson Steer, who had spent some time studying in Paris, was also influenced by Impressionism, particularly by the work of Monet. Steer considered himself an Impressionist (though he finished his paintings in the studio) and at the peak of his career showed an interest in effects of light and weather.

The Italian Antonio Mancini spent some time in Paris between 1875 and 1878, working for the art dealers Goupil and the Dutch painter Hendrik Willem Mesdag. During this period his style became looser, and he tried to achieve rich effects of paint and texture. Mancini's use of color owed much to Venetian painting, but his composition and subjects reflect the impact of Impressionism.

Robert Henri studied at the Académie Julian and the École des Beaux-Arts before returning to the United States. He was influenced by Manet, and then by Thomas Eakins through his pupil Thomas Pollock Anshutz. The Impressionist interest in the themes of everyday life, and a direct, rather sketchy use of paint were dominant in his work.

The German painter, Lovis Corinth, did not conform to any particular style, although he became for a time one of the leaders of German Impressionism. His subject matter followed that of the French painters and he shared their loving observation of the visible world.

d

e

Seurat and Neo-Impressionism

From an early age Seurat was greatly impressed with Delacroix's theories of color. He also studied the work of Pissarro and Monet, and all the available scientific treatises dealing with color, particularly M. E. Chevreul, the early 19th-century scientist, who had suggested that "under simultaneous contrast of colors are included all the modifications that differently colored objects appear to undergo in their physical composition." Seurat was certain that color and composition could be governed by logical method. *Une Baignade*, for which he made many studies (a), was the first painting in which he attempted to carry out his theories. Every aspect of tone, color, and composition was carefully explored.

Seurat used the Impressionist technique as a basis for his method of applying paint, but he applied it with a rigid and mathematical precision. After his meeting with Paul Signac he rejected the use of earth colors and evolved a precise method of arranging primary colors and their complementaries to achieve a proper balance. The separate spots of color were, in theory, to be mixed by the reaction of the spectator's eye.

When Seurat painted *Les Poseuses* (b), he was experimenting with the idea of harmonious lines and surface patterns. The color is in a lower key and applied in finer dots. This was a forerunner of his later canvases in which he was to explore the mathematical relationships in a picture and the symbolism of line and number.

a

b

a Georges Seurat
Study for Une Baignade,
about 1884
oil on panel $6\frac{7}{8} \times 10\frac{3}{8}$ *in.*
Kansas City, Mo., William Rockhill
Nelson Gallery of Art and Mary
Atkins Museum of Fine Arts

b Georges Seurat
Les Poseuses, about 1888
oil on canvas $78\frac{1}{2} \times 98\frac{1}{4}$ *in.*
Merion, Pa., Barnes Foundation

The Neo-Impressionist Movement

Seurat began to codify his ideas on art when he met Signac, and within a short time he had become the acknowledged leader of a new movement which was variously called Neo-Impressionism, Pointillism, and Divisionism. His followers varied in the degree of fidelity with which they accepted his theories. Signac experimented with larger almost uniform, square, brick-like strokes of color. He thus tended to a greater brilliance of color without achieving the subtlety and range of Seurat's work. The task of expounding the theories and of recruiting enthusiasts was undertaken by Signac, and it was he who introduced Pissarro to Seurat in 1885. The older painter, who for some time had been feeling dissatisfied with Impressionism, was searching for a more coherent means of expression. He felt that in Neo-Impressionism he had found the answer. For several years Pissarro humbly followed the lead of the younger painter and helped to spread his theories. There were soon Neo-Impressionist groups all over Europe, Belgium in particular being a flourishing center.

a

b

a Paul Signac
The Entrance of the Port of
Marseilles
oil on canvas
Paris, Musée d'Art Moderne

b Camille Pissarro
River—Early Morning, 1888
oil on canvas   18¼ × 21⅞ in.
Philadelphia, Pa., Museum of Art,
John G. Johnson Collection

Gauguin and Cloisonnisme

The arrival in Brittany of the young painter Émile Bernard in 1888 proved to be the turning point in Paul Gauguin's development. Gauguin had been through an experimental period, influenced by the work of Cézanne and Degas. He was greatly impressed by the austerity and simplicity of Brittany, and sought a completely new kind of art. Bernard showed him his new pictures with their great simplification of form, flat patterns, and heavy black lines (a). This new style had been called "cloisonnisme" because of the way the lines divided up the pictures into compartments as in cloisonné enamels, and had just been evolved in Paris by Bernard and his friend Louis Anquetin.

The intellectual content of Bernard's theories provided an outlet for Gauguin. He decided that "art is an abstraction," that it was unwise to follow nature too closely, and that the painter should think "more of creating than of the actual result. The result should be a synthesis of form and color derived from the observation of the dominant element only." Gauguin felt that it was necessary to achieve a childlike simplicity, to simplify forms and color in order to gain a more forceful expression. He soon surpassed Bernard, and began to use the undulating, rhythmic contour that recurs in so many later paintings. In Arles Gauguin explained to Vincent van Gogh his theory that forms and colors, harmoniously established, produce poetry by themselves.

During Gauguin's stay in Arles his new theories influenced van Gogh, and they painted pictures with similar subject matter (b and c). Gauguin had taken Bernard's *Market in Brittany—Breton Women in the Meadow* (a) with him to Arles, and van Gogh had made a copy of it. This aspect of Gauguin's work had little permanent influence on van Gogh, but it did have a radical effect on a younger generation of painters, who formed the group called the Nabis.

a Émile Bernard
Market in Brittany—Breton
Women in the Meadow, 1888
*oil on canvas 29 × 36 in.
Saint-Germain-en-Laye,
collection Dominique Maurice-Denis*

b Vincent van Gogh
Promenade at Arles—Souvenir of
the Garden at Etten, 1888
*oil on canvas 28¾ × 36 in.
Moscow, Museum of Modern Western
Art*

c Paul Gauguin
Women of Arles, 1888
*oil on canvas 28¾ × 36 in.
Chicago, Art Institute*

a

b

c

Post-Impressionist Developments outside France

Just as the Impressionist idea of painting spread throughout Europe and parts of America, so the effect of Post-Impressionism was felt over a wide field and over a longer period of time. The group called Les XX (which had made Brussels a center of the *avant garde* from 1883) was instrumental in bringing the work of some of the most revolutionary painters to a wider public. The Belgian Théo van

a

b

Rysselberghe was in 1889 converted to Seurat's theories, on which he experimented with personal variations (a). The Pointillist principle was elsewhere often far
more freely adapted. In America, Maurice Brazil Prendergast worked in a mosaic
pattern of small, brightly colored dashes of color (b). His aim was to create
decorative scenes in which nature was merely the starting point for the subject.
Wassily Kandinsky's early work is similar in some respects. In the first decade of
the 20th century he was using small blocks of brilliant color to create landscapes
and evocative illustrations to Russian fairy tales and historical scenes (d). Alexei
von Jawlensky (c), with Kandinsky, was one of the founders of the Blaue Reiter
group. In St. Petersburg and Munich he was influenced by van Gogh, Cézanne,
the Impressionists, and by 1900 he had developed an almost pointillist technique.
He exhibited with the Fauves a few years later, his portrait heads having much in
common with their painting.

c

a Théo van Rysselberghe
Perkiridec Point, 1889
oil on canvas $26\frac{3}{4} \times 41\frac{3}{4}$ in.
Otterlo, Holland, Rijksmuseum
Kröller-Müller

b Maurice Prendergast
The Picnic, 1915
oil on canvas 37×57 in.
Ottawa, National Gallery of Canada

c Alexei von Jawlensky
The Blue Hood
oil on board $25\frac{1}{2} \times 21\frac{1}{4}$ in.
Private Collection

d Wassily Kandinsky
Sunday, Old Russia
oil on canvas $17\frac{3}{4} \times 37\frac{3}{8}$ in.
Rotterdam, Museum
Boymans-van Beuningen

d

Oriental Influences

The Impressionists had been influenced by Japanese art, but their successors the Post-Impressionists were influenced in a more direct way. For van Gogh Japanese art was more than a source of design, it was an emotional reality. He felt that the south of France was Japan, and that in living there he was living in Japan. Often in his letters to his brother Theo he referred to a scene as being "Japanese." He made several copies of Japanese prints (a) and derived from them much of his use of black lines and flat patterns, on clothes and wall-papers, for example, and also the rejection of Renaissance perspective. His many paintings of trees in blossom owe a great deal to Japanese art, and he adopted the symbolism as well as the subjects.

a Vincent van Gogh
Copy after Hiroshige's woodcut,
about 1887
oil on canvas $28\frac{3}{4} \times 21\frac{1}{4}$ in.
Amsterdam, Stedelijk Museum,
V. W. van Gogh Collection

b Ando Hiroshige
Ohashi Bridge in Rain, 1857
polychrome woodcut $14\frac{1}{4} \times 9\frac{3}{8}$ in.
Philadelphia, Pa., Museum of Art, et al.

a

b

Gauguin's style showed an even stronger dependence on Oriental sources. He consciously tried to achieve the directness and strong decorative element that he found in Eastern painting and sculpture. He wrote: "Have always before you the Persians, the Cambodians, and a bit of the Egyptian. The great mistake is the Greek, however beautiful it may be." At the Paris World Fair of 1889 Gauguin visited the Javanese village. He studied photographs of Cambodian and Javanese art (c), longing to go to the tropics in search of new and powerful sensations. One of the results of his studies can be seen in *Ta Matete* (d), in which the stylized, flat forms and delineating outlines common to most Oriental art are predominant. Gauguin's application of eastern elements helped to change the direction of art in the last decade of the 19th century.

c Javanese Temple of Barbudur
(detail of frieze)

d Paul Gauguin
Ta Matete, 1893
oil on canvas $28\frac{3}{4} \times 36$ *in.*
Basel, Öffentliche Kunstsammlung

c

d

The Symbolists

a

The 19th century was a time of remarkable economic and scientific progress and of general prosperity in the middle and upper classes. But the more sensitive artists and poets found the prevailing materialism unsympathetic, and thought that spiritual values were being neglected. They sought an art that would be the opposite of naturalism, an art that would appeal to the imagination and to the senses. Like the writers who shared in this reaction, these artists are often called Symbolists.

This longing for an escape from the present had been manifested early in the century by the German Nazarenes in the form of a nostalgic desire to return to the mysticism of the middle ages. In England, the Pre-Raphaelite Brotherhood represented a comparable movement. Dante Gabriel Rossetti created a dream world, that mirrored a mythical age, drawing on Arthurian legend and medieval romance for its subject matter (a). He derived much of his sensuous, elongated line from a study of William Blake; this in turn became one of the many elements which led to Art Nouveau.

Sir Edward Burne-Jones, who was decisively influenced by Rossetti, also evoked a mysterious dream world, but his forms are more attenuated and brittle (b). In a similar way, the German painter Hans von Marées painted strange monumental compositions inspired mainly by Classical and Renaissance art. His most powerful work was the fresco series painted for the Zoological Institute in Naples (d), in which the life of the local people was transmuted into powerful forms and shapes.

b

c

In Switzerland, Ferdinand Hodler, searching for a formal language that would express esoteric truths (f), evolved a system comprising a rhythmic, repetitive use of line and shape. This "Parallelism" was influenced by the ideas of Gauguin and Seurat, who in certain respects also show symbolist tendencies.

The two French painters most closely associated with Symbolism, however, were Odilon Redon and Gustave Moreau. The latter led a life of seclusion, and depicted curious scenes of biblical and mythological fantasy, encrusted with intricate detail and rich color (c). Redon's forms, unlike Moreau's, are firm and based on a minute study of natural objects. Although they have none of Moreau's langorous quality, they evoke a twilight world, full of implication and sensuous emotion (e).

In all its manifestations Symbolism was an attempt to find a more intense means of artistic expression, a method of evoking the hidden side of life. Art was used to suggest eternal truths instead of representing everyday realities.

a Dante Gabriel Rossetti
How They Met Themselves,
about 1851
pen and ink $10\frac{1}{2} \times 8\frac{1}{4}$ *in.*
Birmingham, England,
City Museum and Art Gallery

b Sir Edward Coley Burne-Jones
Perseus Slaying the Serpent,
about 1875
oil on canvas $60\frac{1}{2} \times 54\frac{1}{4}$ *in.*
Southampton, England, Art Gallery

c Gustave Moreau
Salome Dancing before Herod, 1876
oil on canvas $55\frac{1}{2} \times 41$ *in.*
New York, Gallery of Modern Art,
Huntington Hartford Collection

d

e

f

d Hans von Marées
Men in a Boat (detail)
fresco
Naples, Zoological Institute

e Odilon Redon
Pegasus Captive, about 1908
lithograph
Paris, Bibliothèque Nationale, et al.

f Ferdinand Hodler
A Look into the Unknown, 1915
oil on canvas $175\frac{1}{2} \times 315$ *in.*
Basel, Öffentliche Kunstsammlung

a

Pierre Puvis de Chavannes

Although sometimes associated with the Symbolists, Pierre Puvis de Chavannes belonged to no particular school or trend. He evolved his own highly personal style completely independent of his contemporaries. Of the same generation as the Realists and Impressionists, he was completely unaffected by their work. His ambition was always to paint large decorative schemes for public buildings, and by the 1860's he had achieved a measure of official success. Yet he was always more than just an academic painter, and in the last two decades of the century until his death in 1898 he found himself greatly admired by the younger generation. Both Seurat and Gauguin made copies of his paintings, and the Symbolists and Nabis venerated his work because it seemed to them less superficial and more profound than Impressionism and Realism.

Puvis was essentially a mural painter who worked on a large scale, using drawing and pale fresco-like colors. His primary concern with the bare essentials of form often led to his reducing the picture surface to two dimensions. This interest in flat pattern and allegorical subject matter links him closely with the younger painters of the end of the century.

a Pierre Puvis de Chavannes
Sketch for Death and the Maidens,
about 1872
millboard   16 × 12⅜ in.
London, National Gallery

b Pierre Puvis de Chavannes
The Sacred Grove Dear to the
Arts and the Muses, 1884
oil on canvas   36¼ × 82⅞ in.
Chicago, Art Institute

b

The Nabis

The Nabis, or Prophets, as they called themselves, were a group of very young French painters, who, like the Pre-Raphaelites in England, thought that by banding together they could establish a more imaginative and spiritual art.

Their leader, Paul Sérusier, had met Gauguin in Brittany in 1888, and was inspired to imitate his flat, sinuous, and highly colored style. Like his friend, Maurice Denis, he was of a mystical frame of mind, and later sought the abstract principles which he thought were fundamental to art. Denis was a fervent Roman Catholic with a strong philosophical bent, whose early work, like *April* (b), has a profound poetic melancholy. Pierre Bonnard and Édouard Vuillard, as young men, were also Nabis, and their works show the common influence of Gauguin and Japanese prints with their unusual compositions, flat silhouetted figures, and strong sense of pattern. Bonnard and Vuillard developed a more impressionistic style, sometimes called Intimism because of their preference for interior domestic subjects.

The Nabis were very interested in the applied and useful arts, and in particular made theater designs and posters. Bonnard, like Henri de Toulouse-Lautrec, produced some poster designs in the early 1890's (a) that were to revolutionize this art.

a

a Pierre Bonnard
A Poster for "La Revue Blanche,"
1894
color lithograph 38½ × 23 *in.*
*London, Victoria and Albert Museum,
et al.*

b Maurice Denis
April, 1892
oil on canvas 14¾ × 24 *in.*
*Otterlo, Holland, Rijksmuseum
Kröller-Müller*

b

285

Art Nouveau

In the last years of the 19th century it became very clear that a new style of art was emerging on the international scene. This was called, quite simply, Art Nouveau. Its sources were confusing and varied and included Japanese prints, the English Pre-Raphaelites and William Morris, the Arts and Crafts Movement, the French Symbolists, and certain elements in the work of Gauguin and Toulouse-Lautrec. In *Miss Loie Fuller* (a), for example, Toulouse-Lautrec uses the flat, flowing and flame-like forms that became characteristic of Art Nouveau.

Younger artists all over Europe were working in this new style, often quite independent of one another. The Norwegian Edvard Munch worked mainly in Berlin: his *Madonna* (b) has the undulating forms of the hair, the sinuous twist of the figure, and the sensual undertone common to much Art Nouveau. In his short career Aubrey Beardsley in England revolutionized book design and illustration. In Holland Jan Toorop also did illustration and fabric design: *The Three Brides* (c) shows a clear link with Burne-Jones. Gustav Klimt was the outstanding Austrian exponent of the new style: he made many drawings and adapted

a

b

a Henri de Toulouse-Lautrec
Miss Loie Fuller, 1893
color lithograph $14\frac{3}{8} \times 10$ *in.*
Baltimore, Md., Museum of Art, et al.

b Edvard Munch
The Madonna
color lithograph
Oslo, Nasjonalgalleriet, et al.

c Jan Toorop
The Three Brides, 1893
black chalk $30\frac{3}{4} \times 34\frac{5}{8}$ *in.*
Otterlo, Holland, Rijksmuseum
Kröller-Müller

c

Art Nouveau, or Jugendstil as it was called in Germany, to the demands of monumental painting.

Art Nouveau was not just a new way of painting: it was a European movement in the visual arts that spread to America and affected architecture and every kind of design. In its wider manifestations it included the architects Henri van de Velde and Victor Horta of Belgium, Josef Hoffmann of Austria and Antoni Gaudí of Spain, and Charles Rennie Mackintosh in Britain. Tiffany glass, Liberty fabric designs, and Hector Guimard's Paris Métro Stations are wider manifestations of Art Nouveau.

Many of the practitioners of Art Nouveau, perhaps inspired by the ideas of William Morris, sought expression in other fields of art. Gustav Klimt welcomed the opportunity to adapt his painting for purposes of interior decoration (e), and Mackintosh did not restrict himself only to architecture but designed furniture, every kind of interior fitting, and even the paintings on the walls of his buildings (d). In his work the almost imperceptible movement away from the flame-like, organic forms of the 1890's to the more rectilinear and carefully proportioned art of the 20th century can be seen.

d

e

Index

IMPRESSIONISTS

Names in italics indicate titles
Numbers in italics indicate reproductions
Names in parenthesis indicate locations